SPOTLIGHT

SPOTLIGHT ON GRAMMAR

Arbeitsbuch zur Wiederholung grammatischer Grundstrukturen

NEW EDITION

von Birgit Herrmann

Cornelsen

Vorwort

Spotlight on Grammar ist ein lehrbuchunabhängiges Arbeitsbuch für Klassen der Jahrgangsstufen 8 bis 10, das aber auch zur Unterstützung der Arbeit mit anderen Lehrwerken eingesetzt werden kann. Es dient der Wiederholung und Festigung der wichtigsten grammatischen Strukturen, die in den Klassen 5 bis 7 der Sekundarstufe (Gymnasium, Gesamtschule, Realschule) behandelt wurden. Das Buch eignet sich für Berufsfach- und aufbauschulen, die zum mittleren Schulabschluss führen.

Aufbau und Inhalt

In 24 Units werden die wichtigsten Aspekte der Grammatik im Kontext interessanter und motivierender Themenbereiche behandelt. Die Themen sind der Alltagswelt von Schülerinnen und Schülern entnommen (Beziehungen, Promis, Jobs, Reisen, etc.).

Zu Beginn jeder Unit wird die jeweilige Struktur auf Deutsch erklärt und anhand englischer Beispielsätze veranschaulicht. Anhand der Beispielsätze können die Lernenden die Grammatikregeln überprüfen und sich diese einprägen. Die Hinweise und Beispiele beziehen sich auf die Bildung und Verwendung der zu behandelnden grammatischen Struktur und dienen als Bearbeitungshilfe für die folgenden themengebundenen Übungen. Die Übungen behandeln sämtliche zuvor erwähnten Aspekte des jeweiligen Grammatikthemas – auch kontrastiv.

In vier Tests werden die grammatischen Strukturen der vorausgegangenen Units aufgegriffen, um deren richtige Verwendung überprüfen zu können.

Am Schluss des Buches findet sich eine Liste der wichtigsten unregelmäßigen Verben sowie eine Übersicht über die verschiedenen Zeitformen.

Das Arbeitsbuch ist in zwei Ausgaben erhältlich: mit oder ohne CD-ROM. Auf der CD-ROM befinden sich interaktive Übungen, die von den Lernenden direkt am PC geübt und kontrolliert werden können. Die Übungen beziehen sich auf die Grammatik- und Themenschwerpunkte der Units im Arbeitsbuch.

Verwendungsmöglichkeiten

Spotlight on Grammar eignet sich sowohl zum Selbststudium als auch zur Bearbeitung im Klassenverband. Da die einzelnen Units in beliebiger Reihenfolge bearbeitet werden können, kann das Arbeitsbuch je nach Bedarf eingesetzt werden, beispielsweise zur Vorbereitung von Klassenarbeiten, als zusätzliches Übungsmaterial nach der Einführung eines neuen Grammatikthemas, zur Durchführung von Tests oder zur gezielten Auffrischung lückenhafter Grammatikkenntnisse.

Spotlight on Grammar setzt etwa den bis Ende der Klasse 7 erworbenen Wortschatz voraus. Für schwierigere und eventuell unbekannte Wörter sind Übersetzungen angegeben.

Lösungsheft

Das beigelegte Lösungsheft bietet insbesondere denjenigen Lernern eine Kontrollmöglichkeit, die *Spotlight on Grammar* im Selbststudium bearbeiten.

Wir wünschen Spaß und Erfolg bei der Arbeit mit *Spotlight on Grammar*!

Contents

1 Nouns and articles

A Nouns

1 I like **kiwis**, but I hate **bananas**.
- Die Mehrzahl der meisten Nomen wird mit **-s** gebildet.

2 Can we buy two **boxes** of biscuits, please?
- Endet das Nomen mit -ch, -sh, -ss, -tch oder -x wird **-es** angehängt.

3 Sam's birthday party is at Burger Box. I love **parties**!
- -y (gesprochen wie ein i) wird meist zu **-ies**.

4

man → men woman → women	foot → feet tooth → teeth
child → children person → people	fish → fish sheep → sheep
life → lives	potato → potatoes

- Manche Nomen haben eine besondere Mehrzahlform.

5 My **jeans** are new.
The **news** is on at 8.
- Einige Nomen haben nur eine Mehrzahlform, z.B. *jeans*, *trousers*, *shorts*, *scissors*, *glasses* [Brille] und stehen mit einem Verb im Plural. Wenn man hier eine bestimmte Anzahl meint, benutzt man *pair(s) of*: *two pairs of scissors*. Andere Nomen haben nur eine Einzahlform und benötigen ein Verb im Singular, z.B. *advice*, *homework*, *information*, *news*.

6 This is London**'s** best restaurant.
My parents**'** car is over there.
I don't remember the name **of** the café.
- Der Genitiv wird oft durch das Anhängen von **'s** (= Apostroph + s) angezeigt. Bei Wörtern, die bereits auf -s enden (z. B. Nomen im Plural) reicht der Apostroph (ohne zusätzliches s). Bei Dingen und abstrakten Wörtern sowie bei Maß- und Mengenbezeichnungen benutzt man in der Regel *of*.

B Articles

1 **The** woman with **the** baby can sit on **the** chairs over there.
I can't talk now – I'm **at work**.
- **the** ist der einzige bestimmte Artikel. Anders als im Deutschen wird er oft weggelassen (*by bus*, *after lunch*, *at school*) oder hinzugefügt (*play the guitar*, *in the north*).

2 You need **a** carrot and **an** onion.
I'm going to be **a** baker.
- Der unbestimmte Artikel lautet **a** bzw. **an** (vor Selbstlauten). Er wird auch für Berufs- und Nationalitätsangaben benutzt, z.B. *he's an Australian*, *she's a nurse*.

Eating out

Eating out in London

London is famous for its international restaurants. Many of them offer great meals for under £10. Here are our tips:

1 **Kingsland Road has some excellent Vietnamese cafés. Try their rice noodles with meat.**

2 **Some of the best Turkish restaurants are in Dalston. They're great for fresh salads and vegetables.**

3 **If you want to go out with a large group of people, go to La Porchetta pizzeria. They serve cheap pizzas. (Also good for children.)**

4 **Eat like a king in one of the Indian restaurants on Brick Lane. Their meat or vegetable curries come with rice, two vegetable dishes [*Gerichte*], salad and Indian bread.**

1a *There are 14 plural noun forms in the text. Underline them.*

1b *Find one plural with -es, one plural with -ies and two special plurals and then write their singular form.*

-es: (pl) ____________ (s) ____________
-ies: (pl) ____________ (s) ____________
special: (pl) ____________ (s) ____________
(pl) ____________ (s) ____________

2 *Here are some more tips about eating out in London. Cross out the wrong form.*

1. *Burger / Burgers* are cool again – great for young *peoples / people* who have to be careful with their money. At Hamburger Union you can get them with thick *chip / chips*.
2. Caribbean Flavours has a great *variety / varieties* of Caribbean food and free entertainment every *day / days*. Because of the great music it's also a great place for *parties / partys*.
3. If you like cheap vegetarian *meal / meals*, try Food for Thought. You'll find friendly *waiter / waiters* and fantastic veggie *sandwiches / sandwichs*.
4. Fish is healthy, so go to Fish Club and pick your favourite *fishes / fish*. Their mashed *potatoes / potatos* are a *dream / dreams*!

3 *Complete this breakfast order with the right plural forms.*

Good morning. I'd like to order two full ________ [1] (breakfast) with two ________ [2] (egg), four ________ [3] (sausage), two grilled ________ [4] (tomato), six ________ [5] (piece)[5] of toast, two ________ [6] (glass) of orange juice, two ________ [7] (cup) of coffee and some ________ [8] (strawberry) on the side, please.

4 *Cross out the word which doesn't belong in the group.*

Tip: Think of the plural forms of the words.

1 month, beach, kiss, crash
2 knife, life, wife, sheriff
3 photo, kilo, tomato, radio
4 arm, hand, leg, foot
5 child, kid, son, daughter

5 *Complete the sentences with is or are.*

1 I can't eat out tonight. My jeans ________ too tight [*eng*] already.
2 ________ children allowed in this restaurant?
3 His advice ________ always good – he knows all the best restaurants.
4 What kind of dish ________ that?
5 Where ________ the scissors?
6 The good news ________ that Tim is coming too.

6 *Look at the underlined words in the email below and circle the five genitives.*

New email

Send Chat Attach Addresses Fonts Save

Dear Stacey,

I'm in London now – and it's fantastic! Pam's flat is near the famous Brick Lane, so we often eat out there. I love Indian food! Our neighbours are Indian too. Perhaps they'll show me their country's cooking secrets one day. The markets here sell lots of different Indian things, and the music's great! The tourists' cameras are always busy. Pam says she's getting fed up with tourists – except me, of course! Tonight we're going to London's best restaurant for young people. Wait for it – it's called Hamburger Union!

Lots of love,
Vanessa

PS I haven't been to your cousin's house yet, although it's not far from here. I'll call her as soon as possible.

7 *Complete the sentences using the genitive of the words in brackets.*

1 Hamburger Union is the ________ (children) favourite restaurant.
2 I was hungry so I finished my ________ (parents) meals too.
3 We went to that restaurant for dinner on ________ (Peter) birthday.
4 The ________ (men) toilets are at the back of the café.
5 ________ (Jess) cake was bigger than mine.

8 *a or an? Fill in the right article.*

1 ____ banana	5 ____ onion	9 ____ nut
2 ____ apple	6 ____ mushroom	10 ____ egg
3 ____ orange	7 ____ tomato	11 ____ cake
4 ____ kiwi	8 ____ carrot	12 ____ ice cream

9 *Complete the sentences with an article (a/an or the) where needed.*

1 I'd like to be ____ chef [*Koch/Köchin*]. I want to be on ____ TV one ____ day.
2 I'm looking for ____ summer job as ____ waitress. I've worked in ____ restaurant before. It's ____ fun.
3 My ____ father is ____ baker. It's ____ good job, but he doesn't like getting up early.
4 Perhaps I can work as ____ assistant in the local café in ____ July. It's easy to get there by ____ bus.
5 I've always done a lot of ____ writing at ____ school. My ____ dream is to be ____ restaurant critic, you know, writing about ____ restaurants. I'd love that.
6 I'm not very good at ____ maths or English. But I love ____ cooking. I hope I can work as ____ kitchen assistant later.

2 Pronouns A

A Personal pronouns

1 **I • you • he/she/it • we • you • they**
me • you • him/her/it • us • you • them
I like Sam. Sam likes **me**.

- Personalpronomen kommen in zwei Formen vor: als **Subjektform** (*I*, etc.) oder als **Objektform** (*me*, etc.). Die Objektform steht nach einem Verb oder nach einer Präposition (*with her*, *behind us*, *next to them*).
- Anders als im Deutschen (mir/mich etc.) gibt es im Englischen nur **eine** Objektform (*me*, etc.).

2 **You** drive on the left in Britain.

- Das Pronomen *you* kann auch „man" bedeuten.

3 Is that a new skirt? I really like **it**.

- Anders als im Deutschen (er, sie, es, usw.) verwendet man immer *it*, wenn man von Dingen spricht.

B Possessive forms

1 **my • your • his/her/its • our • your • their**
mine • yours • his/hers/– • ours • yours • theirs
That's **my** bag. It's **mine**.

- Es gibt zwei Arten von Possessivgebrauch: vor einem Nomen (*my*, etc.) bzw. vor einem Nomen mit Adjektiv (*my old bag*) und **anstelle** eines Nomens (*mine*, etc.), wenn man das Nomen nicht wiederholen will (*That's a great bike. Is it ~~your bike~~ yours?*). Aufgepasst: Kein Apostroph bei Possesivformen.

2 Pam has broken **her** leg.

- Statt eines Artikels gebraucht man im Englischen ein Possessivpronomen, wenn man über Körperteile spricht.

C Reflexive pronouns

1 **myself • yourself • himself/herself/itself**
ourselves • yourselves • themselves
I hurt **myself**.

- Bei bestimmten Verben braucht man ein Reflexivpronomen, z. B. *cut*, *enjoy*, *hurt*, *teach*, *wash*. Sie entsprechen ungefähr „sich (selbst)", werden aber z.T. mit anderen Verben verwendet. Aufgepasst: Einige englische Verben brauchen im Gegensatz zum Deutschen **kein** Reflexivpronomen, z. B. *break (a leg)*, *hide*, *remember*.

2 We made these bags **ourselves**.

- Mit einem Reflexivpronomen kann man auch betonen, dass jemand etwas selbst gemacht hat.

3 Anna and Bill looked at **themselves** (*sich*) in the mirror.
Anna and Bill looked at **each other** (*einander, sich gegenseitig*).

- Beachte den Unterschied.

Swishing (1)

"Swishing? What's that? Oh, I know! A party where people can swap [*tauschen*] clothes, isn't it?"

"My friend and I went to a swishing party. It was so much fun – we really enjoyed ourselves. And we got some fantastic dresses that we really like."

"I hate to throw away good clothes. Swishing parties are a great way to give away clothes and feel better about yourself."

"My sister is a student, so she doesn't have much money. As soon as she saw this black dress she said, 'That's mine!'"

"I went there with two pairs of new shoes that I had never really liked. I went away with a lovely winter coat that I needed."

1 ***Underline all the pronouns. Use red for personal pronouns (15), blue for possessive pronouns (3) and green for reflexive pronouns (2).***

2 ***Imagine you're Rosie and write down which pronouns you have to use.***

1 Rosie got an invitation to go to a swishing party and take as many of her old clothes as possible.

I, ______________________

2 Rosie picked a skirt and a pair of jeans that had never really fitted [*passten*] her. Then she went to the party.

____

3 She really enjoyed herself. A woman tried Rosie's jeans on and she looked great in them. Rosie said that the jeans used to be hers.

____

4 Rosie found a great jacket for herself. It really suited her and now she wears it all the time.

____

3 Cross out the wrong personal pronoun.

1 I went to a swishing party with *she* / *her* (my sister).

2 Sarah invited *we* / *us* (my friend and me).

3 I didn't see *they* / *them* (Fatima and Joe).

4 She really likes *him* / *it* (that coat).

5 I've always wanted *them* / *it* (those jeans).

6 This jacket belongs to *him* / *he* (Paul).

4 Complete the text with the right pronouns.

I've just washed ________________ [1] hair for the party and am ready to go. We're going to be late though because Peter hasn't brushed ________________ [2] teeth yet. My sister has broken ________________ [3] arm so she can't come to the party tonight. I'm going to take ____________ [4] coat with ________________ [5] though for her because she really wanted to swap ________________ [6] and get a new bag. Maybe I'll find something nice for her there.

5 Match the parts of the sentences.

1	I bought	a	ourselves in the mirror.
2	My friends enjoyed	b	myself a new coat.
3	Amy made	c	hurt yourself?
4	We looked at	d	themselves at the swishing party.
5	My brother laughed at	e	herself a new skirt.
6	Did you	f	himself.

6 Complete the text about ways to save money with the right pronouns.

Teenagers never have enough money. So how do ________________ [1] deal with this problem? **TEEN** asked readers for ________________ [2] personal money-saving tips:

We don't often go to the cinema. ________________ [3] parents give ______________ [4] DVDs for ______________ [5] birthdays, and then ________________ [6] have DVD parties. Tina, 15

Our comment: Yes, but do ________________ [7] really enjoy ________________ [8]?

I buy second-hand things on the internet a lot – computer games, books and so on. For ________________ [9], that's an easy way of saving money. Adam, 16

Our comment: Internet auctions are fun and a good way to save money.

The girls here love swishing parties. ________________ [10] take unwanted clothes and find things which really suit ________________ [11] – for nothing! Jamie, 18

Our comment: Clothes swapping is mega-in! ____________ [12] save money and ________________ [13] have fun at the same time – ________________ [14] favourite!

7 Similar but different! Put the right word in the right space.

1 (their; they're) Teenagers don't have much money. ________________ always trying to save. Some of ________________ money-saving ideas are really good.

2 (it's; its) Pam got a great dress at the swishing party. ________________ the perfect dress for her, and she just loves ________________ colour.

3 (you're; your) I always buy and sell things on the internet. If ________________ getting a new bike for your birthday, I could sell ________________ old bike there.

4 (there's; theirs) I never check how my daughters spend their pocket money. They can do what they like with it – it's ________________ . And ________________ not a lot I can do anyhow.

3 Pronouns B

A Demonstrative pronouns

1 **This** car here is ours.
That bike over there is Sam's bike.
These shirts cost £5. **Those** are £10.

- Mit den Demonstrativpronomen *this* (Plural: *these*) und *that* (Plural: *those*) weist man auf etwas hin. Meist benutzt man *this (these)* für Dinge, die näher dran sind, und *that (those)* für weiter Entferntes.

2 **This** is the cheap shop – **that**'s the expensive boutique.
I like **these** shoes better than **those**.

- Demonstrativpronomen werden oft benutzt, um Gegensätze anzuzeigen.

B One /ones

1 That's my coat over there. – Which **one**? – The black **one**.
There are two sorts of cakes. The big **ones** are cheaper than the small **ones**.

- Mit dem Stützwort *one* kann man ein bereits verwendetes Nomen ersetzen. So vermeidet man Wortwiederholungen. Für Nomen im Plural verwendet man *ones*.

2 Both colours look great. **Which one** do you prefer?
I'd like that shirt, please. – **This one** or **that one**?

- *one/ones* wird oft nach *which, this* oder *that* verwendet.

3 Tim has a new pen. – Is it an **expensive one**?
Have you seen the new lights? I preferred the **old ones**.

- *one/ones* wird oft in Verbindung mit einem Adjektiv benutzt.

Watch out!

Das Stützwort *ones* ist eine Pluralform und braucht keinen Apostroph!

Swishing (2)

1 ***Cross out the wrong form.***

1 I hate *this / these* jeans. They look terrible!
2 Could you give me four of *these / those* bananas, please?
3 *This / That* is my favourite pair of shoes.
4 Can you see *this / that* dress over there?
5 I'll take two pullovers to the swishing party: this *one / ones* here and that *one / ones* there.

2 ***Rewrite the underlined parts of the sentences. Use one/ones where possible.***

1 Which coat suits me better – <u>this coat or that coat</u>?

___

2 I'm looking for dresses. <u>Where can I find the best dresses?</u>

___

3 Look, these shoes don't go together. <u>This is a black shoe and that's a blue shoe.</u>

___

4 I took <u>two old skirts and a new skirt</u> to the swishing party.

___

5 Where's the letter? – <u>Which letter? The letter that Paul wrote or the letter from school</u>?

___

3 ***Translate the sentences. Use pronouns and one/ones wherever possible.***

1 Dies ist Ellas Fahrrad. Und das da ist ihr Mantel.

___

2 Die Häuser hier sind alt. Die Häuser da drüben sind neu.

___

3 Ich mag diese Kleider lieber als jene dort.

___

4 Diese CDs kosten £10 und die dort £15.

___

Spotlight on …
Word order

Ella likes music.
I work because **I need the money**.
- Die Wortstellung im Englischen ist genau festgelegt: **Subjekt – Verb – Objekt**, auch im Nebensatz.

A Place and time

1 I went **to the party**.
We have lunch **at school**.
- Ortsangaben stehen in der Regel am Ende des Satzes.

2 Tim bought a coat in town **yesterday**.
Last week I saw an interesting article in the newspaper.
- Zeitangaben können ganz am Anfang oder am Ende des Satzes stehen.

3 I went **to the party on Thursday.**
- Ortsangaben kommen vor Zeitangaben.

4 My friend **often** sells things on the internet.
I can **always** find something interesting.
I'm **usually** bored at parties.
- Häufigkeitsangaben wie *always, often, usually, sometimes, never* stehen meist direkt vor dem Hauptverb. Sie stehen aber nach dem Verb *to be*.

B Sentences with two objects

1 I've given *my brother some clothes.*

- Nach dem Verb steht, *wem* etwas gegeben/gezeigt/… wird. Danach steht, *was* gegeben/gezeigt/… wird.

2 I've given *some clothes* **to** *my brother*.
- *Wem* etwas gegeben/gezeigt/… wird, kann man auch mit **to** am Ende des Satzes sagen.

1 *Choose the best possible place for the adverbs.*

Danny is really good with money – but Paula is really bad …

1 (never) Paula [ ] has any money [ ].
2 (always) She [ ] spends [ ] everything she gets.
3 (sometimes) But Danny [ ] saves [ ] his money.
4 (usually) He [ ] spends [ ] very little.
5 (often) So Paula [ ] tries to borrow money [ ] from Danny.
6 (never) But Danny says no because he knows he'll [ ] get it [ ] back.

2 *Is the word order in these sentences right [✔] or wrong [✘] ? Correct the wrong sentences.*

1 [ ] My friends and I organised a flea market last year.

____

2 [ ] Around the youth club we put our things on some tables.

____

3 [ ] A great success was it!

____

4 [ ] We sold the teenagers lots of our old CDs and DVDs.

____

5 [ ] "It's great that we can buy here cheap things," they said.

____

6 [ ] We gave to a church project part of the money.

____

4 The verb 'be'

A Simple present

1

I am	you are	he/she/it is	we are	you are	they are
I'm	you're	he's/she's/it's	we're	you're	they're

I **am** 16.
You**'re** too young.

- Im *simple present* hat das Verb *be* die Formen *am, are* und *is*. Diese werden sehr oft als Kurzformen gebraucht. Wichtig: Kurzformen werden immer mit Apostroph geschrieben!

2 The club is **not** open for everybody.
You're **not** young enough for the club.

- Die Verneinung wird mit *not* gebildet.

3 **Is** Gavin English? – Yes, he **is**. / No, he**'s not**.
Are you happy? – Yes, I **am**. / No, **I'm not**.

- Fragen werden durch Umstellung von Verb und Subjekt gebildet. Entscheidungsfragen werden oft mit Kurzantworten beantwortet.

B Simple past

1

I	you	he/she/it	we	you	they
was	were	was	were	were	were

I **was** in London last week.
Mick and Joe **were** unhappy after the party.

- Im *simple past* hat das Verb *be* die Formen *was* und *were*.

2 Pam **was not** at the party.

- Die Verneinung wird mit *not* gebildet (Kurzformen: *weren't/wasn't*).

3 **Were** you late for the party?

- Auch im *simple past* werden Fragen durch Umstellung von Verb und Subjekt gebildet.

C There is/are ...

There's a new club. **There are** lots of people inside.
There was a new DJ at the club yesterday.

- Mit *there is (there's)* und *there are* drückt man aus, dass etwas vorhanden ist *(simple past: there was/were)*. Diese Formulierung entspricht etwa dem Deutschen *es gibt/gab* bzw. *es ist/sind/war/waren*.

Watch out!

Es gibt = There is/are ... NOT ~~It gives ...~~

Cool clubbing for teens

Cool clubbing

There is a new club in town. But it is not for everybody. Once a month the Martinique opens its doors for a special crowd. They are young, they are cool and they want to dance. There is a live band and a DJ, but there is not any alcohol. The doors open from 4 o'clock – in the afternoon. And there are checks at the door because not everybody can get into this new club. Here is the secret: it is only for teens between 14 and 18. They are the people who are too young to go to normal discos – and they love the underage club.

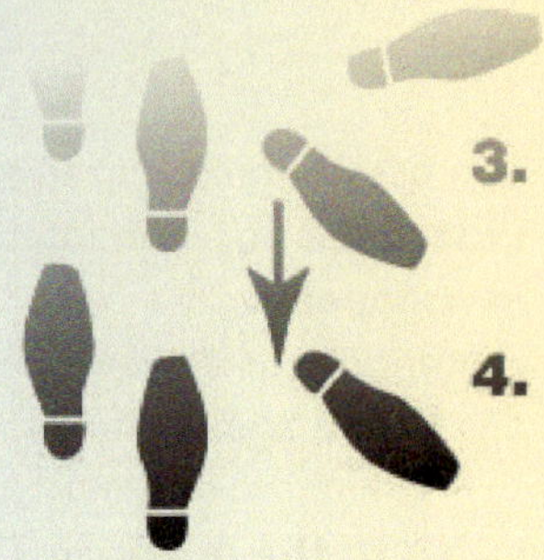

1 ***Find 10 long forms of the verb be and write down their short forms.***

__________ __________ __________
__________ __________ __________
__________ __________
__________ __________

2 ***Complete the text with the right form of be.***

The organizer, Vanessa, __________ [1] under 18 herself. She __________ [2] surprised that so many teens love it – and that there __________ [3] lots of bands who want to come and play at the club.
The bands __________ [4] also young themselves but they __________ [5] already famous and mega-cool.
Ryan, 17, often goes to the club. He says: "The music __________ [6] fantastic and I love it that there __________ [7] no alcohol around." And the parents? "It __________ [8] a wonderful idea." says Ryan's mother. "There __________ [9] finally something that our kids love doing – and they __________ [10] safe doing it."

3 Match the parts of the sentences.

1	The underage club	a	are really happy about it.
2	The underage kids	b	aren't too young there!
3	They	c	is a fantastic idea.
4	There	d	am so happy about the club.
5	Their parents	e	aren't worried about them there.
6	I	f	isn't any alcohol in the club.

4 Complete the sentences about Vanessa and Rick. Use the right form of *be*.

1 Rick's hair *is* brown.
Vanessa's hair ________________ brown,
it ________________ blonde.

2 Rick's eyes ________________ blue.
Vanessa's eyes ________________ blue,
they ________________ brown.

3 Rick ________________ tall.
Vanessa ________________ tall,
she ________________ small.

4 Rick: "Vanessa, you ________________ 18, right?
You ________________ 17, like me."
Vanessa: "No, I ________________ 17.
I ________________ 16!"

5 Complete the short answers.

1 Is the underage club for everybody? – No, *it isn't*.
2 Are the kids in the underage club under 18?
– Yes, ________________ .
3 Vanessa, are you older than 18?
– No, ________________ .
4 Ryan, are you 17? – Yes, ________________ .
5 Is it an alcohol-free club? – Yes, ________________ .
6 Are the parents unhappy? – No, ________________ .

6 Complete Aysha's story. Use *was, were, wasn't* or *weren't*.

Last summer I ________________ [1] in a club with my older sister. I ________________ [2] old enough yet, but I used a lot of make-up and looked older. There ________________ [3] a band there that I really wanted to see. The club ________________ [4] very full. A lot of the women ________________ [5] really drunk [*betrunken*]. They laughed a lot, but they ________________ [6] very funny! I ________________ [7] happy and I couldn't enjoy the music. Suddenly there ________________ [8] some drunk men around me. They said stupid things and wanted me to drink their beer. I ________________ [9] really frightened. Then my sister came and we left. I ________________ [10] quite shocked.

7 Write questions about an underage festival in Victoria Park, London. Use the simple past.

1 the festival / be / a success
Was the festival a success?

2 there / be / lots of cool bands?
____

3 there / be / thousands of fans?
____

4 the fans / be / loud?
____

5 there / be / anybody over 18 there?
____

6 the organizer / be / happy?
____

8 Cross out the wrong verb.

1 There *was / were* seven stages [*Bühnen*] in Victoria Park.
2 There *was / were* lots of great bands.
3 There *was / were* some short films too.
4 There *was / were* a lot of singing and dancing.
5 There *was / were* some great food as well.

5 The verb 'have'

A Simple present

1 I **have** a bike.
My sister **has** a laptop.
- Im *simple present* ändert das Verb *have* seine Grundform nur in der dritten Person: *he/she/it has*.

2 We **do not have** a car.
He **doesn't have** a computer.
- Die Verneinung wird mit *do not* (Kurzform: *don't*) oder *does not* (Kurzform: *doesn't*) gebildet; darauf folgt immer die Grundform *have*.

3 **Do** you **have** enough money? – Yes, I **do**. / No, I **don't**.
Does Al **have** red hair? – Yes, he **does**. / No, he **doesn't**.
- Fragen und Kurzantworten werden mit *do/does* (+ *have*) gebildet.

4 We**'ve got** a house.
Sue **has got** long hair.
- Statt *have* kann auch *has/have got* (Kurzform: *'s/'ve got*) gebraucht werden, wenn man über Besitz spricht. Es wird allerdings nur im *simple present* benutzt.

5 My brother **hasn't got** a job.
Have you **got** a hobby? – Yes, I **have**. / No, I **haven't**.
- Verneinung, Fragen und Kurzantworten werden bei der Verwendung von *have got* nicht mit *do/does*, sondern mit *have/has* gebildet.

B Simple past

1 I **had** a great holiday.
He **had** a lot of fun.
- Im *simple past* hat das Verb *have* die Form *had*.

2 Paul **didn't have** much fun.
Did Jo **have** a good time? – Yes, she **did**. / No, she **didn't**.
- Für Verneinung, Fragen und Kurzantworten benutzt man Umschreibungen mit *did* (+ Grundform *have*).

E-pals

Hi, I'm Dennis. I'm 15 years old. I'm tall and I have blonde hair[1] and blue eyes. We have got a flat[2] in Hamburg and I go to school there. I have a digital camera[3] and I like taking photos. I also like cats and dogs, but I don't have a pet[4]. My parents say I can't have one, because we haven't got a garden[5]. I'm often very busy but I always have time to write[6]. I'd like to have an e-pal [*Internet-Brieffreund/in*] from Britain.

1 ***Sharon saw this advert and is telling her friend about Dennis. Put the underlined phrases in the right form.***

1 *He has blonde hair.*
2 ______
3 ______
4 ______
5 ______
6 ______

2 ***Complete these questions. Use have or have got.***

1 ______ brothers or sisters?
2 ______ a best friend?
3 ______ your friend ______ e-pals too?
4 ______ a favourite band?
5 ______ your own bedroom?
6 ______ your flat ______ a balcony?

3 ***Complete the sentences. Use the right form of have not.***

1 That's wrong! Dennis ______ brown hair.
2 That's wrong! His parents ______ a house.
3 That's wrong! Dennis ______ a dog.
4 That's wrong! His parents ______ a garden.

4 *Write sentences with have. Think about the tense.*

1 Laura / have / 10 e-pals

____

2 I / not have / as many e-pals as Laura

____

3 I / have got / 6 e-pals

____

4 I / only / have / 4 e-pals / last year

____

5 My e-pal Jason / have / a new dog

____

6 He / not have / a dog when I started writing to him

____

5 *Match the questions with the right short answers from the box.*

a Yes, he did.	b Yes, they did.
c Yes, they have.	d Yes, he does.
e Yes, they do.	f Yes, he has.

1 Do your friends have e-pals too? [ ]

2 Does Dennis have your email address? [ ]

3 Did Jennifer and her friend have a nice holiday? [ ]

4 Has Dennis got a computer in his room? [ ]

5 Have his parents got good jobs? [ ]

6 Did Dennis have a party for his birthday? [ ]

6 *Look at the table and answer the questions with the right short answer.*

	Melinda	Murat	Bina	Kevin
dog	✓	✗	✗	✗
bike	✗	✓	✗	✓
mobile phone	✓	✓	✓	✓
MP3 player	✗	✗	✓	✓
laptop	✓	✗	✗	✗

1 Does Melinda have a dog? _______________

2 Has Murat got a mobile phone? _______________

3 Has Bina got an MP3 player? _______________

4 Do Kevin and Bina have a laptop? _______________

5 Have Murat and Kevin got a bike? _______________

7 *Correct these sentences. One of them is already correct.*

1 My brother have an e-pal.

____

2 Have you an e-pal?

____

3 My sister had a good time last night.

____

4 Did Sue have a good holiday? Yes, she had.

____

5 We had got a house but we have now got a flat.

____

8 *Now read the email that Sharon wrote to Dennis and complete the questions. Use the simple past.*

New email

Send Chat Attach Addresses Fonts Save

Hi Dennis,

We had so much fun on holiday! We had a really good break. We got up late in the mornings and had a shower before we had breakfast at 11. Then we went down to the pool and had a drink (or two). After that we had lunch. We had a good chat with the other guests. In the afternoon we often had an ice cream on the beach. And in the evenings there was always somebody who had a party!

And what about you? How was your holiday? _______________ you _______________ [1] a good break? When _______________ [2] breakfast in the mornings? _______________ [3] drinks at the pool too? _______________ [4] lots of chats with other guests? Where _______________ [5] your ice cream – on the beach? And _______________ they _______________ [6] lots of parties as well?

9 *There are many special phrases with have. Match the phrases from Sharon's email with their German translation.*

1 have a break	a etwas trinken
2 have a chat	b ein Eis essen
3 have a drink	c sich unterhalten
4 have a party	d Pause machen
5 have a shower	e eine Party geben
6 have an ice cream	f frühstücken
7 have breakfast	g (zu) Mittag essen
8 have lunch	h duschen

6 Simple present

A Positive statements

1 Superstars **earn** a lot of money.
He **earns** £5,000 a month.
My daughter **watches** every superstar show on TV.
Every time he **tries** to dance, he **falls** over.

- Die Form des Verbs im *simple present* entspricht seiner Grundform. Nur in der dritten Person (*he/she/it*) wird ein *-s* angehängt (*-es* nach *-ch/-sh/-ss/-tch/-x* und *-ies* nach Mitlaut + *y*).

2 Lou **does** Mel's make-up.
He **goes** to all the shows.

- Beachte die Ausnahmen.

B Negative statements

I **do not live** in London.
Mike **doesn't eat** meat.

- Die Verneinung wird mit *do not* (Kurzform: *don't*) oder *does not* (Kurzform: *doesn't*) gebildet; darauf folgt **immer** die Grundform (also die Form ohne *s*-Endung!).

C Questions and short answers

1 **Do** you often **fly** to New York? – Yes, I **do**. / No, I **don't**.
Does Tammy **smoke**? – Yes, she **does**. / No, she **doesn't**.

- Fragen werden mit *do* oder *does* und der Grundform (ohne *s*-Endung!) gebildet.

2 What **do** you **eat** for breakfast?
How **does** he **prepare** for a show?

- Auch Fragen mit Fragewörtern bildet man mit *do/does* + Grundform.

3 Who **sings** that song?
What **makes** you sad?

- Nur wenn *who* oder *what* anstelle des Subjekts stehen, braucht man keine Umschreibung mit *do/does*.

D Usage

Pat goes to Australia **every year**.
I **never** go to bed after 10 o'clock.
John doesn't speak German.

- Mit dem *simple present* spricht man über regelmäßige Handlungen, Gewohnheiten und Allgemeingültiges. Es wird oft mit Zeit- und Häufigkeitsangaben verwendet (z. B. *every week, on Mondays, often, usually, sometimes, never, etc.*).

Superstars

Who wants to be a superstar?

YES!
"I want to be a superstar. Superstars don't worry about money. They spend a lot of time with other superstars. They live in big houses and drive big cars. They don't work a lot. They just smile and earn more money."
(Miguel, 15)

NO!
"I don't want to be a superstar. A superstar always worries about his or her looks [*Aussehen*] and everybody criticizes your clothes and your make-up. Nobody tries to see the person behind the image. A superstar doesn't lead a normal life. He or she never gets any peace."
(Daisy, 16)

1 ***Underline the verbs in the simple present. Use red for the infinitive form, blue for third person s and green for the negative form.***

2 ***They all want to be superstars. Complete the sentences using the verbs in the box.***

act • cook • dance • play • sing

1
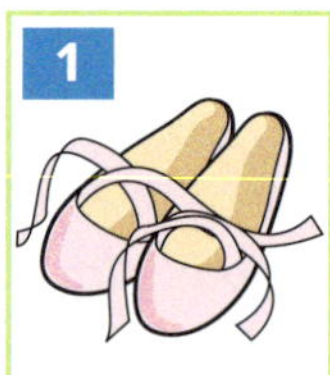
2

3

4

5

6

1 Sophie *dances*.
2 Robbi ______________________.
3 Mustafa and Paolo ______________________.
4 Kim ______________________.
5 Mel ______________________.
6 Gordon and Julie ______________________.

My day as a superstar by Simon (14)

I wake up late in the morning. I don't get up – I have breakfast in bed. I listen to some music and then I take a walk around my garden. I swim in the pool for a while. Then I call my driver and I get into a big white car. I do some shopping in town and I give lots of autographs [Autogramme]*. I don't worry about the money that I spend because I have enough. In the evening I meet some interesting rich people for dinner and I go to bed really late.*

3 ***Write an article about Simon. Put all the verbs in the third person.***

Simon, the superstar
He wakes up late in the morning. He doesn't get up ...

____

____

____

____

____

____

____

____

4a ***Simon writes to his favourite star and asks him about his life. Write questions with do or does.***

1 you always get up late?

____

2 your butler make your breakfast?

____

3 you have a big pool?

____

4 your driver do other jobs too?

____

5 you ever worry about money?

____

4b ***Now complete the star's short answers.***

1 No, ________________ . I usually have lots of work.
2 No, ________________ . I don't have a butler!
3 Yes, ________________ . Swimming keeps me fit.
4 Yes, ________________ . He's always busy.
5 No, ________________ . I pay somebody else to worry about it.

5 ***Complete the questions about being a football star. Decide if you have to use do.***

1 (have to) How often *do I have to* train?
2 (need) What kind of help ________________?
3 (have) Who ________________ the best manager?
4 (make) What ________________ the fans angry?
5 (prepare) How ________________ for an important match?
6 (earn) How much money ________________?

6 ***Write sentences about the real life of superstars.***

1 get up / often / early in the morning / they
They often get up early in the morning.

2 keep / have to / they / always / fit

____

3 drink / never / alcohol / most of them

____

4 be / often / away from home / an actor / for months

____

5 train / usually / for five hours / a day / a football star

____

6 have / once a year / but / a great holiday / they

____

7 ***Odd word out. Cross out the word that doesn't belong in the group.***
Tip: Look at the rules for the third person s again.

1 mix, eat, switch, pass
2 tries, buys, pays, says
3 matches, finishes, writes, fixes
4 moves, smokes, changes, misses
5 apply, stay, fly, worry
6 watches, guesses, leaves, relaxes

7 Present progressive

A Positive statements

1 I'**m waiting** for an answer.
The phone **is ringing**.

- Man bildet das *present progressive* mit einer Form von *be* (*am/is/are*; auch als Kurzform) und der *-ing*-Form des Verbs.

2 I'm si**tt**ing in front of my computer.
Andy is wri**t**ing an email.

- Infinitivendungen wie *-m*, *-n* oder *-t* werden nach kurz gesprochenen Silben verdoppelt (z. B. *sit, swim, begin, run, get, put*). Ein stummes *-e* am Ende des Infinitivs (z. B. *write, drive, make, ride, use*) fällt in der *-ing*-Form weg.

B Negative statements

Pamela is **not** using her computer at the moment.
We are**n't** talking right now.

- Die Verneinung wird mit *not*/Kurzform gebildet.

C Questions and short answers

Is Ben **playing** a video game? – Yes, he **is**. / No, he **isn't**.
What **are** you **doing**?

- Um eine Frage zu bilden, stellt man Hilfsverb und Subjekt um. Das gilt auch für Fragen mit Fragewörtern.

D Usage

1 I can't come now – I'm **just** having a chat with Jill.
It isn't raining **now**.

- Mit dem *present progressive* sagt man, was gerade jetzt oder vorübergehend (nicht) geschieht (z. B. *just, still, at the moment, now*).

2 I'm going to the cinema **soon**.
We're playing football **later**.

- Mit dem *present progressive* (normalerweise mit Zeitbestimmung) kann man auch über feste Pläne und Verabredungen sprechen.

Watch out!

Für Verben wie *like, love, want, hate, believe, understand* und *know* wird in der Regel **nicht** das *present progressive* verwendet: *Ah, now I understand you!*

Always in touch

Can somebody help me, please?!?

I can't. I'm talking to John on my mobile phone.

Sorry, Nikki can't. She's just writing an email upstairs.

No, we can't. We're watching TV at the moment.

Sorry, Tom can't. He's chatting online right now.

Luke and Lisa? Sorry, they can't. They're just surfing the internet.

OK. I'm not doing anything right now. What's the problem?

I'm looking for my mobile ...

1 ***Underline the verbs in the present progressive above. Which one is in the negative?***

2 ***At the school camp. Circle the right -ing form.***

1 Don't worry, Mum. I'm not *smokeing / smoking* or *drinkking / drinking*. It's not allowed.
2 You aren't *missing / mising* much. It's boring here.
3 Jack isn't *surffing / surfing* the internet now. He is *geting / getting* ready to go swimming.
4 I hope he's not *spending / spendeing* too much money at the camp.
5 They're just *writeing / writing* a postcard now.

3 ***It's happening soon! First circle the correct verb form and then match the sentence parts.***

1	Hurry! The train *am leaving / is leaving*	a	to London today?
2	I *am flying / is flying*	b	at the weekend.
3	We *am working / are working*	c	another laptop tomorrow.
4	My parents *am getting / are getting*	d	a big party on Friday.
5	Our firm *is having / are having*	e	to Spain on Saturday.
6	*Am you going / Are you going*	f	in three minutes.

4 *Complete the sentences with the present progressive.*

1 He ______ (check) his emails.
2 She ______ (talk) on her mobile phone.
3 She ______ (call) a customer.
4 We ______ (take) pictures.
5 They ______ (put) photos on the internet.
6 I ______ (write) a text message.

5 *Complete this chat with the present progressive of the verbs in brackets.*

Hi, Chris. How are things back in England?
I ______ [1] (sit) at a youth hostel computer at the moment. So answer me NOW!

Hi, Rachel! Wow! ______ [2] (you write) from Australia? That's cool! So what ______ [3] (you do) over there?

I ______ [4] (enjoy) life – Australia is just awesome! ______ [5] (it rain) in England?

Of course it ______ [6] (rain)! What did you expect?

Well, it ______ [7] (not rain) here! It's sunny and I ______ [8] (go) to the most fantastic beach in a moment.

You ______ [9] (make) me jealous! When ______ [10] (you come) back?!

I don't know. I ______ [11] (meet) so many interesting people here. I might stay longer ;-) Look, I'm sorry but I have to go now because somebody else ______ [12] (wait) to use the computer. See you soon!

6 *Look at each answer and complete the questions. Use the verbs from the box.*

do • go • have • rain • speak

1 What ______ at the moment? – I'm just writing an email to a customer.
2 Where ______? – Oh, Danny is just walking into town for lunch.
3 Sorry, who ______ to? – It's Jem Buck speaking.
4 When ______ lunch? – Now! I'm hungry!
5 ______ at the moment? – No, it isn't raining. Let's go.

7 *Write sentences using the present progressive.*

1 I / read / your email / at the moment
______
2 She / call / me / soon
______
3 you / talk / to Sharon / later / ?
______
4 I / look at / your photos / now
______
5 The phone / still / ring
______
6 it / snow / in Canada / now / ?
______

8 *Underline the time phrases that are typical for the present progressive.*

1 Can I borrow your MP3 player? – No, I'm just listening to the new Blue CD.
2 Are you leaving now? – Yes, my mum is waiting for me.
3 Can I call you back? I'm just chatting with Lou.
4 Isn't Pat using the computer at the moment? – No, she isn't. She's having lunch.
5 He said he would phone me on Tuesday. I'm still waiting for that phone call.

Contrast: Simple present ▸◂ present progressive

(▸ S. 14–17)

Adam **plays** *the guitar.* ▸ ◂ *Adam* **is playing** *the guitar.*

Mit dem *simple present* spricht man über regelmäßige Handlungen, Gewohnheiten oder Allgemeingültiges. Mit dem *present progressive* sagt man, was gerade jetzt geschieht oder was fest geplant oder verabredet ist.

Watch out!

Verben wie *like, love, want, hate, believe, understand* und *know* werden in der Regel nur im *simple present* verwendet.

1 ***Cross out the wrong verb forms.***

1 Hurry! The bus *is coming / comes*. It only *is coming / comes* once an hour.

2 *We're playing / We play* table tennis at the youth club on Mondays. Tonight *we are playing / we play* against a team from Bristol.

3 My sister often *is sending / sends* texts to her friends. Look, *she's writing / she writes* one now.

4 *I'm driving / I drive* to London this afternoon. *I often go / I'm often going* to London.

5 My parents *are working / work* in a factory. But *they aren't working / they don't work* at the moment – *they're watching / they watch* TV.

6 My father *is cooking / cooks* – that means *we're eating / we eat* soon.

2 ***Complete the sentences using the simple present or present progressive. Then write the verbs in the puzzle to find a signal word for the simple present.***

1 Look! Those ducks *are swimming* (swim) in our pool!

2 Pam ____________________ (usually do) her homework at school.

3 I ____________________ (never read) books. I hate it.

4 I ____________________ (go) into town now. What about you?

5 Natalie ____________________ (still wait) for an answer.

6 A baker ____________________ (sell) bread and cakes.

7 Our dog often ____________________ (lie) on his back.

8 I ____________________ (play) the guitar in a concert later.

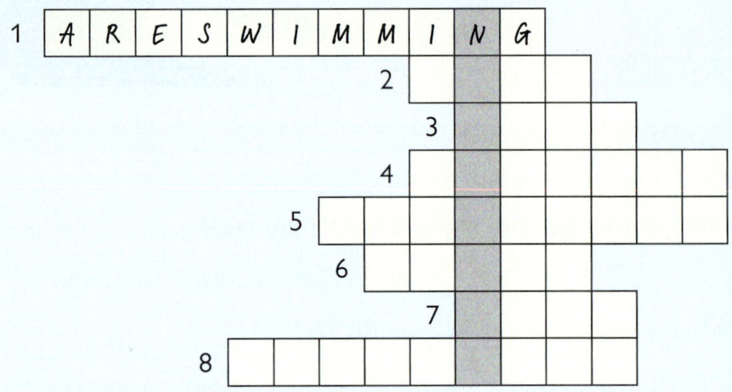

3 ***Write sentences using either the simple present or the present progressive.***

1 She / always / eat / breakfast at 7

____

2 It / snow / at the moment

____

3 I / love / the summer

____

4 you / come / to the cinema with us / tomorrow / ?

____

5 the train / leave / at 4 o'clock

____

6 I / can / not talk / now. I / wash / my hair

____

Test 1

Nouns and articles (▸ S. 4)

1 ***Complete the sentences with the English translation of the German words in brackets.***

1 I'd like to have a shop that sells ________________ (*Zeitungen*) and ________________ (*Zeitschriften*).

2 They've got two new vegetarian ________________ (*Gerichte*), but I'll have my favourite cheese ________________ (*belegtes Brot*) again.

3 My favourite ________________ (*Hobbys*) are cycling and swimming, but I also do lots of other ________________ (*Aktivitäten*).

4 I have two ________________ (*Brillen*) but I still can't find my ________________ (*Hose*)!

5 All this ________________ (*Hausaufgaben*) and I can't find the ________________ (*Informationen*) that I need anywhere on the internet!

2 ***Tick [✔] the right box to complete the sentences.***

		a	an	the	no article
1	My sister is going to be … teacher.	✔			
2	Can we meet after … lunch today?				
3	I'm looking for … American e-pal.				
4	I'd like … apple, please.				
5	My father is still at … work.				
6	Amy lives in … north of England.				
7	Bill is coming by … train.				
8	I'd like one of … oranges over there.				

Pronouns A (▸ S. 6)

3 ***Find the right pronoun for each sentence and put it in the crossword.***

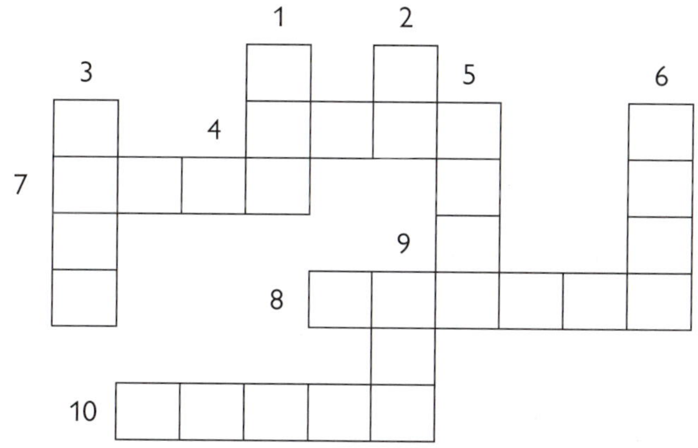

1 Nice toy bear! What's … name?

2 I like going out with you. Can … go out again soon?

3 I like … new jacket, Tom.

4 Pete and Rick are here. Let's dance with … .

5 Give it back! It's not your mobile, it's … !

6 Jane bought Bill's bike. It's … now.

7 We saved money for a long time. Now the house is … .

8 Look at my parents' new car – the green one is … .

9 My brother has some nice clothes. This is … shirt.

10 Emma, are these jeans mine or are they … ?

Pronouns B (▸ S. 8)

4 ***Complete the sentences. Use this, that, these, those, one or ones.***

1 ________________ is my coat over there, the pink ________________ .

2 ________________ here is my dog, that ________________ is Lilly's.

3 I like ________________ jeans better than the black ________________ over there.

4 ________________ houses down there are nice.

5 I like ________________ shirt here best. Which ________________ is your favourite?

6 Which cake should I have: ________________ strawberry cake here or ________________ chocolate one over there?

Word order (▸ S. 9)

5 ***Decide where the missing part of the sentence has to go.***

1 (yesterday) I found [ ] an advert in the paper [ ].
2 (need) I'm looking for a job because I [ ] the money [ ].
3 (tomorrow) [ ] I'm going [ ] for a job interview.
4 (on the internet) I want to buy myself [ ] a used laptop [ ].
5 (always) But laptops are [ ] quite [ ] expensive.
6 (me) My brother can't lend [ ] the money [ ].
7 (already) He [ ] gave [ ] some money to my sister.
8 (at the weekend) I went [ ] to the cinema [ ].
9 (my sister) I sent [ ] an email [ ] but she still hasn't replied.
10 (often) I [ ] am [ ] at home earlier than my brother.

The verb 'be' (▸ S. 10)

6 ***Match the parts of the sentences.***

1	Lots of teenagers	a	is really friendly. I like her.
2	Mike	b	're my best friend.
3	She	c	are often bored.
4	I	d	is famous for its churches.
5	You	e	am English.
6	The town	f	isn't hungry at the moment.

7 ***Complete the sentences with there is/are/was/were (not).***

1 ______________ about 30 people in the room when we arrived.
2 ______________ always snow in the winter in Austria.
3 I had to go to the shop because ______________ enough potatoes left.
4 ______________ so many things I want to see!
5 Sorry I'm late. ______________ an accident in town.
6 ______________ many girls in our class. Only about six, I think.
7 ______________ often interesting birds to see.
8 ______________ a piece of cake for everybody.

The verb 'have' (▸ S. 12)

8 ***Read the text and cross out the wrong verb forms.***

My friend Pamela *has / have / don't have*[1] red hair. She *doesn't have / don't have / had*[2] any problems with that. But last year she *had / has / have*[3] a boyfriend who wasn't very happy with it. He said: "All your friends *don't have / have / had*[4] blonde or brown hair. Why don't you?" They *doesn't have / had / have*[5] a big row [*Streit*]. She shouted: "Look at you! You *didn't have / doesn't have / don't have*[6] any hair at all!" In the end he left. She *had / has / have*[7] a new boyfriend now – it's her hairdresser!

9 ***Complete the dialogue with the right form of have.***

A Paul ______________[1] a new bike.
B Another one? How many bikes ______________[2] now?
A Three. His parents ______________[3] lots of money.
B And he ______________[4] a job.
A I ______________[5] a great bike too. But it was stolen. I still ______________[6] enough money to buy a new one though.

10a ***Write the questions.***

1 you have any brothers or sisters?
____

2 you have a good holiday last year?
____

3 you have got a laptop?
____

4 you have time to help me with my homework?
____

10b ***Now match the short answers to the questions you have written above. One of them goes with two questions.***

a Yes, I have. [ ] [ ]
b Yes, I do. [ ] [ ]
c Yes, I did. [ ] [ ]

Simple present (▸ S. 14)

11 *Write questions in the simple present. Think about whether or not you need a question word.*

1 ____ ?

Yes, I like my job as a hairdresser.

2 ____ ?

No, I don't earn enough money!

3 ____ ?

Yes, my boss gives me enough help.

4 ____ ?

The customers think it's great to see a boy in this job.

5 ____ ?

I enjoy talking to the customers most.

6 ____ ?

It makes me happy to see happy customers.

7 ____ ?

I don't like working on Saturdays.

8 ____ ?

Yes, I get two days off during the week.

12 *We're all different! Tick [✓] the right negative form.*

		don't	doesn't	
1	I	✓		like meat.
2	Rachel			eat fruit.
3	My sisters			drink milk.
4	Mike			read books.
5	I			like comics.
6	He			buy magazines.
7	We			listen to the radio.
8	Our dog			like music.

Present progressive (▸ S. 16)

13 *Fill in the table with the right -ing form. Decide where in the table you have to put it.*

		just -ing	without -e	double letter
1	write		*I'm writing*	
2	win			
3	visit			
4	use			
5	try			
6	take			
7	swim			
8	smile			
9	sleep			
10	run			

14 *Complete the dialogue. Choose between the simple present and the present progressive.*

Sue: Hi, Lydia. What ____________________ [1] (you do)?

Lydia: Hi, Sue. I ____________________ [2] (write) an email at the moment.

Sue: Interesting. I ____________________ [3] (never use) a computer in my job. I ____________________ [4] (have to) talk to people all day.

Lydia: But that's great! I often ____________________ [5] (get) really bored just working on the computer. I ____________________ [6] (listen) to the radio right now but that's boring too. I ____________________ [7] (only see) other people at lunch.

Sue: Well, I ____________________ [8] (meet) the girls for a drink after work. ____________________ [9] (want) to come too?

8 Simple past

A Positive statements

1 Batman appear**ed** for the first time in 1939.
He tr**ied** to stop crime.
Readers lik**ed** the new superhero.
He pla**nned** to catch criminals.

- Regelmäßige Verben werden im *simple past* durch das Anhängen von **-ed** an die Grundform gebildet (**-ied** nach Mitlaut + *y*). Ein stummes -e am Ende des Infinitivs (z.B. *decide, phone, use, like*) fällt weg. Infinitivendungen wie *-n, -p, -r* oder *-t* werden oft verdoppelt (z.B. *plan, prefer* [vorziehen], *stop*).

2 Batman soon **became** very popular.
He **did** a great job.

- Unregelmäßige Verben haben besondere Formen, die gelernt werden müssen (vgl. Liste auf S. 67). Viele der häufig verwendeten Verben sind unregelmäßig (z.B. *do, go, get, become*).

B Negative statements

I **did not watch** Batman last night.
Libby **didn't read** Batman comics when she was young.

- Die Verneinung wird mit *did not* (Kurzform: *didn't*) gebildet; darauf folgt immer die Grundform (also die Form ohne -*ed*-Endung!), deshalb ist hier die Unterscheidung zwischen regelmäßigen und unregelmäßigen Verben nicht nötig.

C Questions and short answers

1 **Did** you **buy** these comics? – Yes, I **did**. / No, I **didn't**.
What **did** you **like** most about the film?

- Fragen werden mit *did* und der Grundform gebildet. Das gilt auch für Fragen mit Fragewörtern.

2 Who **played** Batman in the last film?

- Nur wenn mit *who* oder *what* nach dem Subjekt gefragt wird, braucht man keine Umschreibung mit *did*.

D Usage

I watched the new film **last week**.
His parents died **when he was a child**.
First I bought the DVD. **Then** I watched it.

- Mit dem *simple past* spricht man darüber, was zu einem bestimmten Zeitpunkt oder in einem bestimmten Zeitraum geschah. Dabei verwendet man oft Zeitangaben wie *yesterday, last week/..., two days/... ago, in 2008*. Das *simple past* benutzt man auch, wenn man eine Abfolge von Ereignissen in der Vergangenheit schildert.

Batman

I watched a Batman film last week. It was really interesting. It told the story of how Bruce Wayne became Batman. Bruce really loved his parents, who were rich people, but a criminal killed them while he was still a child. When he grew up, he saw how crime really hurt a lot of people in his home town, Gotham. So one day he began to fight against the criminals. He didn't have superpowers like Superman so he used some clever things to help him, like his bat *[Fledermaus]* costume and the 'batmobile' (his special car). When Batman discovered that his teacher was really one of the criminals who planned to destroy *[zerstören]* the city, he fought him and won. I really enjoyed the action scenes in the film. I read some Batman comics when I was younger but I thought the film was much better.

1 ***Find all the simple past forms. Underline the regular verbs in blue and the irregular verbs in red.***

2 ***Complete the sentences with the simple past of the verbs in brackets.***

1 I ____________ (collect) Batman comics when I was younger.
2 I always ____________ (want) to buy them as soon as they came out.
3 I ____________ (love) the stories where Batman fought against the Joker.
4 My brother ____________ (prefer) Superman to Batman.
5 We often ____________ (watch) them on DVD together.
6 Our parents always ____________ (worry) that we watched too many DVDs!
7 I often ____________ (play) with Batman toys.

3 ***Complete the sentences with the simple past of the verb in brackets in the negative form.***

1 My sister ______________ (like) Batman.
2 She ______________ (have) any Batman comics.
3 We ______________ (play) together much.
4 She ______________ (want) to watch the movies.
5 She ______________ (try) to understand me.
6 I ______________ (enjoy) playing with her.

4 ***Match the verbs.***
Tip: Think of the simple past forms.

1 jog, fit, drop, …	a carry
2 apply, copy, dry, …	b write
3 celebrate, admire, agree, …	c plan
4 play, stay, enjoy, …	d test
5 come, hide, make, …	e destroy
6 jump, print, offer, …	f cycle

5 ***Write the simple past form of the verbs in the crossword.***

1 sing	4 keep	7 give
2 lose	5 spend	8 drive
3 know	6 eat	9 put

6 ***First cross out the wrong simple past form. Then complete the sentences with the negative of the same verb.***

1 Bruce Wayne *telled / told* his butler that he was Batman.
He ______________ anybody else.
2 The people of Gotham *knowed / knew* that Batman fought criminals. They ______________ he was a normal man.
3 Batman's costume *maked / made* him look like a huge bat.
It ______________ him stronger.
4 The Joker *followed / follew* Robin. He ______________ Batman.
5 The criminals *saw / seed* a big, dark shadow [*Schatten*].
They ______________ Batman coming.

7 ***Complete the questions.***

1 ______________ you ______________ the Batman DVD?
– Yes, we did. We bought it last month.
2 ______________ Tom ______________ the film?
– Yes, he did. He liked it very much.
3 What ______________ the criminals ______________ ?
– They stole important plans.
4 Where ______________ Batman ______________ after the fight?
– He went to Hong Kong.
5 ______________ Batman ______________ ?
– Yes, he won.

8 ***Write sentences in the simple past.***

1 Batman / decide / to fight crime when he / be / young
____
2 the criminals / kill / a lot of people
____
3 you / read / Batman comics when you / be / at school /?
____
4 my brother / buy / a Batman DVD yesterday
____
5 a new Batman movie / come out / a few years ago
____
6 Darren / watch / the new movie with you / ?
____
7 we / go / to see the film in the new cinema
____
8 it / be / a very good film
____

9 Present perfect

A Positive statements

The reporter **has** talk**ed** to the teachers.
The teachers **have given** interviews already.

- Das *present perfect* wird mit dem Hilfsverb *have/has* (Kurzformen: *'ve* und *'s*) und dem *past participle* gebildet. Bei regelmäßigen Verben hat das *past participle* dieselbe Form wie das *simple past* (Grundform + *-ed*). Bei unregelmäßigen Verben ist es eine weitere besondere Form des Verbs (vgl. Liste auf S. 67).

B Negative statements

The police **have not arrived** yet.
The school **hasn't called** the police.

- Die Verneinung wird mit *have/has not* (Kurzformen: *haven't/hasn't*) und dem *past participle* gebildet.

C Questions and short answers

Have you **phoned** him yet? – Yes, I **have**. / No, I **haven't**.
What **has** she **told** the reporter?

- Um eine Frage zu bilden, stellt man *has/have* und das Subjekt um. Das gilt auch für Fragen mit Fragewörtern.

D Usage

1 I've warned the teachers.
He has **just** pulled a gun out of his bag.
We've helped pupils **before**.

- Mit dem *present perfect* sagt man, dass
  – etwas gemacht/erledigt worden ist (ohne Zeitangabe)
  – etwas gerade eben geschehen ist (*just*)
  – etwas schon einmal gemacht wurde (typische Adverbien: *already, always, before, ever, never*).

2 We've known them **since the summer**.
They've been in the school **for two hours**.

- Mit dem *present perfect* sagt man auch, wie lange etwas schon andauert (*since* = Zeitpunkt; *for* = Zeitspanne). Anders als im Deutschen verwendet man im Englischen nicht das *simple present*: *She has lived here since 2005.* [Sie lebt seit 2005 hier.]

Watch out!

1 try ▶ t**ried**; like ▶ lik**ed**; jog ▶ jo**gg**ed (vgl. S. 22)
2 Das *present perfect* wird immer mit *have/has* und nie mit einer Form von *be* gebildet – also kann *he's arrived* nur *he* **has** *arrived* bedeuten!

A school shooting

"This is Radio KFM. Thank you for listening. We've just heard that a man with a gun has hurt at least one person in a school shooting *[Schulamoklauf]* this morning. We've sent our reporter to the school – Jim?"
"Yes, hello, Susan. It's a terrible scene here at the moment. I've never seen anything like this before. The police haven't given us any details yet. All we know is that a young man has killed at least one person. It seems that he has also injured four others. The first ambulance has just arrived. Police have gone into the building. Many students have escaped to a nearby church but we can't talk to them yet. Somebody said that police have arrested the man, but this hasn't been confirmed *[bestätigt]* yet."

1 ***Underline all the present perfect forms in the text and then complete the table below with verbs from the text.***

	infinitive	*simple past*	*present perfect*
1			I've heard
2	hurt		
3			I've sent
4		I saw	
5	give		
6		I killed	
7	arrive		
8		I went	

2 ***Read sentences 1-3 and tick the sentence (A or B) which means the same.***

1 Mr Thomas has taught at the school since 2003.
[ ] A Mr Thomas works at the school now.
[ ] B Mr Thomas doesn't work at the school now.

2 I've always thought that guns are a problem.
[ ] A I used to think guns are a problem.
[ ] B I still think guns are a problem.

3 The police have been in the building for hours.
[ ] A The police are in the building.
[ ] B The police aren't in the building.

3 ***Complete these comments using the present perfect.***

I ______________________ [1] (just come) out of the building. I can't talk yet.

I ______________________ [2] (follow) the reports about school shootings for several years. But I didn't think it would happen to us.

I ______________________ [3] (have) a bad feeling about him since I came to this school.

I ______________________ [4] (not tell) anyone about this yet but I knew he had a gun.

School ______________________ [5] (always be) easy for me. But it was terrible for him.

4 ***Two hours after the shooting. Complete the sentences using the negative.***

1 The school has cancelled [*abgesagt*] lessons for the rest of the week.

______________________________ lessons yet.

2 Police have announced a press conference for this afternoon.

______________________________ a press conference yet.

3 A reporter has put videos about the shooting on the internet.

______________________________ on the internet yet.

4 The school has asked a therapist [*Therapeut/in*] to help the children.

______________________________ a therapist to help the children yet.

5 We have heard the latest news.

______________________________ the latest news yet.

5 ***Write the questions and then complete the short answers.***

1 you ever have trouble with guns at this school?

____

No, ______________________ . Everything was fine.

2 the school be in the news before?

____

Yes, ______________________ . But it was always good news!

3 you speak to other reporters yet?

____

No, ______________________ . I've just come out of the building.

4 you and your class ever discuss school shootings?

____

Yes, ______________________ . But I never thought it would happen here.

5 you see the therapist yet?

____

No, ______________________ . I think I'm fine.

6 ***For or since? Cross out the wrong word.***

1 The shooter has been in the building *for / since* two hours now.
2 Police have known about the shooting *for / since* 8 a.m.
3 The students have been in the school *for / since* hours. The police will help them soon.
4 More and more parents have arrived *for / since* the end of the shooting.
5 The reporters have taken lots of photos *for / since* they arrived.
6 John has been at this school *for / since* the summer.

Contrast: Simple past ►◄ present perfect

(► S. 22–25)

I **worked** *here last summer.* ►◄ *I've* **worked** *here for two years.*

Mit dem *simple past* spricht man über abgeschlossene Vorgänge in der Vergangenheit. Mit dem *present perfect* sagt man, was (gerade) geschehen ist, was schon einmal gemacht wurde und wie lange etwas schon andauert; das Geschehen hat Auswirkungen auf die Gegenwart.

1 ***Write down the time phrase from each sentence and tick whether the sentence is in the simple past (s.p.) or the present perfect (p.p.).***

1 My brother repaired my bike last weekend.
2 We've lived here for about five years.
3 The teacher told them about the test last Monday.
4 I've had this mobile since May 15th.
5 James has played the guitar for seven years.
6 They sent me a letter two months ago.

	When?	Since when?	For how long?	s.p.	p.p.
1	*last weekend*			✔	
2					
3					
4					
5					
6					

2 ***Cross out the wrong tense.***

1 *I just finished / I've just finished* an email to Sue.
2 *We bought / We've bought* a new car last year.
3 *I never heard / I've never heard* such a good song before.
4 Jill *lived / has lived* in Germany for a year in 2006.
5 Great! Joe *already made / has already made* the coffee.
6 First *we played / we've played* basketball. Then we *had / we've had* lunch.
7 *Did you ever see / Have you ever seen* Dracula?
8 *We were / We've been* in London since 2004.

3 ***Translate the sentences using the simple past or the present perfect.***

1 *Toll – Emma hat Eis mitgebracht!*
Great – Emma ______________________ some ice cream.

2 *Als ich die Schmerzen im Bein hatte, hat mich mein Vater überall hingefahren.*
When I had the pain in my leg, my dad
____________________________ me everywhere.

3 *Ich habe nur 5 Pfund für mein neues Handy gezahlt.*
______________________ five pounds for my new mobile.

4 *Ich erwachte mitten in der Nacht.*
____________________________ in the middle of the night.

5 *Ich habe heute morgen Cornflakes zum Frühstück gegessen.*
___________________________ for breakfast this morning.

6 *Ich fahre jetzt seit zwei Stunden mit meinem Fahrrad.*
______________________ my bike _________________ .

7 *Meine Eltern haben mir etwas mehr Geld gegeben.*
____________________________ me some more money.

8 *Ich habe noch nie so viel Geld ausgegeben.*
____________________________ so much money.

9 *Wir wohnen in Hamburg seit fünf Jahren.*
____________________________ five years.

10 *Ich habe Bauchschmerzen. Ich habe seit zwei Tagen Bauchschmerzen.*
___________________ stomachache. _________________ .

10 Past progressive

A Positive statements

At six o'clock yesterday I **was doing** my homework and my parents **were watching** TV.

- Man bildet das *past progressive* mit *was* oder *were* und der *-ing*-Form des Verbs.

B Negative statements

The boy was **not** running when he fell.
We were**n't** listening when the teacher explained our homework.

- Die Verneinung wird mit *not* (bzw. einer Kurzform) gebildet.

C Questions and short answers

Were you **reading** when Laura came? – Yes, I **was**. / No, I **wasn't**.
What **was** Sam **doing** when you saw him?

- Um eine Frage zu bilden, stellt man das Hilfsverb und das Subjekt um. Das gilt auch für Fragen mit Fragewörtern.

D Usage

1 What **were** you **doing** at 1 o'clock yesterday? – I **was having** lunch.

- Mit dem *past progressive* sagt man, was zu einem bestimmten Zeitpunkt gerade (nicht) geschah.

2 We **were eating** when the phone **rang**.

- Mit dem *past progressive* sagt man, was im Gange war, als etwas anderes plötzlich geschah *(simple past)*.

3 While you **were sleeping**, I **was watching** TV.

- Mit dem *past progressive* spricht man über Handlungen, die gleichzeitig abliefen; beide Handlungen stehen im *past progressive*.

Watch out!

Bei der Bildung der *-ing*-Form werden Infinitivendungen wie *-m*, *-n* oder *-t* nach kurz gesprochenen Silben verdoppelt; ein stummes *-e* am Ende des Infinitivs fällt weg (vgl. *present progressive*, S. 16).

www.SailMike.com

Mike Perham is now the youngest person who has sailed *[segelte]* around the world alone. After 22 months of preparation *[Vorbereitung]*, the 16-year-old left Portsmouth in England for his trip around the world.

1 ***What was happening when Mike's boat left Portsmouth? Match the sentence parts.***

1	The photographers	a	was blowing.
2	His sister was so sad, she	b	was shouting goodbye.
3	His team manager	c	was crying.
4	Lots of people	d	were clapping their hands.
5	The wind	e	were taking photos.

2 ***During the trip Mike wrote a blog about his experiences. Put the verbs in the right form (past progressive or simple past).***

1 While I ______ (sail) south yesterday, I was writing my blog.

2 I was having dinner when I ______ (notice) that the wind had changed.

3 I ______ (take) photos of the dolphins when my camera broke.

4 The boat ______ (move) up and down while I ______ (try) to fix the sails [*Segel*].

5 Just when I ______ (fall asleep) again, the alarm clock ______ (go) off.

3 ***Fans around the world sent Mike their questions. Write his answers.***

1 What was your sister doing when you were getting ready to leave?
(cry) ______

2 What were you doing when it started to rain yesterday?
(have breakfast) ______

3 Were you sleeping when the storm started?
(yes) ______

4 Were you looking forward to stopping in South Africa?
(no) ______

5 What were you doing when you noticed the whale [*Wal*]?
(write blog) ______

11 Past perfect

A Positive statements

The girl **had looked** for a job for a long time when she saw the advert.
I stopped looking for a job after **I'd found** this one.

- Das *past perfect* wird mit dem Hilfsverb *had* (Kurzform: *'d*) und dem *past participle* gebildet. Bei regelmäßigen Verben hat das *past participle* dieselbe Form wie das *simple past* (Grundform + *-ed*).
  Bei unregelmäßigen Verben ist es eine besondere Form des Verbs (vgl. Liste auf S. 67).

B Negative statements

The ambulance **had not arrived** when the boss came in.

- Die Verneinung wird mit *had not* (Kurzform: *hadn't*) und dem *past participle* gebildet.

C Questions and short answers

Had you **checked** the machine before you turned it on?
– Yes, I **had**. / No, I **hadn't**.
What **had** her boss **told** her before she started work?

- Um eine Frage zu bilden, stellt man Hilfsverb und Subjekt um. Das gilt auch für Fragen mit Fragewörtern.

D Usage

After I **had worked** for two hours, I **needed** a break.
When I **arrived**, Angela **had** already **left** the club.

- Mit dem *past perfect* kann man zeigen, dass ein Ereignis in der Vergangenheit weiter zurückliegt *(past perfect)* als ein anderes *(simple past)*.

Watch out!

1 try ▶ tr**ied**; like ▶ lik**ed**; jog ▶ jo**gged** (vgl. S.22)
2 Das *past perfect* wird im Englischen immer mit *had* gebildet, auch wenn es im Deutschen nicht „hatte" sondern „war" heißt:
*he **had** gone* (= er war gegangen).

Safety at work

The lost finger

Emma had looked for a summer job for weeks when she finally saw an interesting advert in the paper. She applied for it and she got the job: 8 weeks work in a bakery! She had been very happy because she really needed the money for a new computer.
Emma had only been at work for about an hour when the accident happened. A machine pulled her left hand into it after she had tried to take some bread from the machine's rotating table *[Karussell]*. She had pressed the off button *[Aus-Knopf]*, but the machine was broken. The doctors in the hospital hadn't asked her before they cut off a part of her finger.
Emma's boss tried to find out what had gone wrong. Here's what he found:
- Emma had not had the right training on the machine.
- The other workers had known for two weeks that the machine was broken.
- Nobody had told Emma that the machine was broken.

1 ***Underline the past perfect forms in the text above. Use red for irregular verbs and blue for regular verbs.***

2 ***Complete Emma's story with the past perfect of the verbs in brackets.***

1 I ________________ (come) into the bakery the day before to introduce myself.

2 After the manager ________________ (give) me my work clothes, I started work.

3 When I ________________ (prepare) everything for the machine, I switched it on.

4 The manager ________________ (tell) me to take the pies off the rotating table after 12 minutes so that's what I did.

5 Although I ________________ (press) the off button, the machine didn't stop.

3 *Poor Luke! What went wrong? Complete the sentences using the simple past and the past perfect.*

1 He *fell off* (fall off) the roof because he *had gone* (go) too far up.

2 He ________ (drive) off the road because he ________ (not see) the warning sign.

3 He ________ (hurt) his head because he ________ (not put on) his helmet.

4 He ________ (burn) his hand because he ________ (forget) the machine was hot.

5 He ________ (hurt) his knees because he ________ (not use) the right safety equipment.

6 He ________ (break) his arm because he ________ (not read) the safety instructions [*Sicherheitsvorschriften*].

4 *Read the questions and complete the short answers.*

1 Had you checked the oil before you drove the car?
Yes, ________ .

2 Had you filled the car up with petrol before you returned it?
No, ________ .

3 Had you read the instructions before you started the machine?
Yes, ________ .

4 Had you put on gloves before you cut the meat?
No, ________ .

5 Had you tried the soup before you served it?
No, ________ .

5 *My first day at work. Put in the past participles and then match the sentences.*

1	Yesterday I was tired because	a	I ________ (not work) at a machine before.
2	I was nervous yesterday because	b	I ________ (not have) time for lunch.
3	I was happy last night because	c	I ________ (make) a mistake.
4	I was angry in the afternoon because	d	I ________ (do) well on my first day.
5	I was hungry when I got home because	e	I ________ (get) up so early.

6 *What happened first? Join the sentences together using the past perfect. You will need to use one of the words in the box.*

after • because • so • when

1 The workers started. Mike arrived.
The workers had started when Mike arrived.

2 Sue forgot to wear a helmet. She hurt her head.
____

3 Mark listened carefully. He did well.
____

4 Phil washed his hands. Then he prepared the food.
____

5 Suzi cut the vegetables. Then she put the vegetables in the fridge.
____

6 First Jane turned on the machine. Then she put in the pies.
____

7 Mike forgot to turn the computer off. Joe did it.
____

8 Sarah went to work. Then the postman came.
____

12 Future

A The will future

1 It **will be** (It **'ll be**) spring soon.
- Diese Zukunftsform wird mit *will* und der Grundform des Verbs gebildet. Die Kurzform von *will* lautet *'ll*.

2 The shops **will not** (**won't**) be open later.
- Die verneinte Form lautet *will not* (Kurzform: *won't*).

3 **Will** you **miss** school? – Yes, I **will**. / No, I **won't**.
What **will** happen next?
- Um eine Frage zu bilden, stellt man Verb und Subjekt um. Das gilt auch für Fragen mit Fragewörtern.

4 My sister **will be** 16 in May.
Please come soon. I think **you'll like** it here.
I'll carry that for you.
- Diese Zukunftsform wird vor allem benutzt, um
  – sichere Vorhersagen zu machen,
  – Vermutungen über Zukünftiges zu äußern und
  – spontane Angebote/Entscheidungen zu formulieren.

B The going to future

1 We**'re going to make** a cake today.
- Diese Zukunftsform wird mit einer Form von *be* (*am/is/are*; auch als Kurzform) + *going to* sowie der Grundform des Verbs gebildet.

2 She **isn't going to wear** that dress.
- Die Verneinung wird mit *not*/Kurzform gebildet.

3 **Are** you **going** to cook today? – Yes, I **am**. / No, I**'m not**.
What **is** she **going** to buy him?
- Um eine Frage zu bilden, stellt man Hilfsverb und Subjekt um. Das gilt auch für Fragen mit Fragewörtern.

4 **I'm going to be** a firefighter.
We**'re going to play** tennis later.
Look at the sky! It**'s going to rain** soon.
- Diese Zukunftsform wird vor allem benutzt, um
  – (Berufs-)Pläne/Absichten zu formulieren oder
  – über unmittelbar bevorstehende Ereignisse zu sprechen, für die es bestehende Vorzeichen gibt.

C Present progressive and simple present

1 **I'm working** tomorrow.
- Absichten und Vorhaben kann man auch mit dem *present progressive* formulieren.

2 The train **leaves** at 7 a.m.
- Das *simple present* wird für feste Termine wie Stunden- oder Fahrpläne verwendet.

Caring about the climate

1 ***Complete the text with the will future.***

Have you heard about the greenhouse effect *[Treibhauseffekt]*? It *will probably change* (probably change) our world forever. Here are some predictions *[Vorhersagen]*:

1 The greenhouse effect ______________ (bring) higher temperatures of between 1.5 – 4.5° Celsius by the year 2030.

2 Our winters ______________ (get) warmer and warmer.

3 It ______________ (make) the world hotter than it has been for more than 100,000 years.

4 Hurricanes ______________ (become) stronger.

5 In summer more land ______________ (dry out).

2 ***Write sentences about people's predictions about cars. Use the will future.***

1 there / only be / small cars

____

2 there / not be / as many fast cars

____

3 cars / cost / much more

____

4 you / have to pay / much more for fuel

____

5 there / still be / too many cars on the road

____

6 all cars / use / electricity

____

7 more people / share / cars

____

8 people / not drive / cars any more

____

3 ***Before the hurricane (1). Complete the sentences with the right verb from the box in the will future.***

check • keep • know • listen • protect • put

The Kelly family live in Florida. There are lots of hurricanes there but they know what they will have to do when one starts:

1 Everybody ______________________ to the news carefully.

2 Mr and Mrs Kelly ______________________ their windows with wood.

3 They ______________________ enough petrol in the car.

4 Their daughter Pam ______________________ all important papers in waterproof containers [*Behälter*].

5 She ______________________ if there's enough food and water in the house for at least three days.

6 Everybody ______________________ where to go if they have to leave their home.

4 ***Before the hurricane (2). Complete the sentences using the going to future.***

A hurricane is on its way to Florida. The Kellys have to act fast. This is what they plan to do:

1 Pam ______________________ (buy) some more water.

2 Mr and Mrs Kelly ______________________ (put) wood in front of the windows.

3 They ______________________ (not wait) any longer.

4 Pam ______________________ (take) everything in from outside.

5 She ______________________ (not forget) the bicycles.

5 ***Complete the sentences with the will or going to future.***

1 Scientists think that our winters ______________________ (get) warmer and warmer.

2 We ______________________ (collect) rubbish at the beach tomorrow.

3 We've decided that we ______________________ (use) recycled paper from now on.

4 I ______________________ (not drive) to school anymore. I think it ______________________ (be) better to walk.

5 You think that car sharing is a good idea? I ______________________ (share) a car with you.

6 ***Simple present or present continuous? Circle the best future form.***

1 The environment conference *starts / is starting* at 10 a.m. tomorrow.

2 Steven *goes / is going* to the conference in the morning. He *takes / is taking* the train.

3 The train *leaves / is leaving* at 8 a.m. and *arrives / is arriving* at 9.30.

4 Steven *gives / is giving* a presentation on a new car sharing scheme in the afternoon.

5 His presentation *finishes / is finishing* at 6 p.m.

6 Afterwards he *goes / is going* to dinner with a colleague.

7 ***Translate these sentences. Use the best future form.***

1 Wissenschaftler denken, dass der Treibhauseffekt die Erde wärmer machen wird.

____

2 Morgen besuche ich eine Umweltkonferenz.

____

3 Der Zug kommt heute Abend um 19.00 Uhr an.

____

4 Ich werde Wissenschaftler wenn ich älter bin.

____

5 Ich fahre nächstes Jahr nach Spanien.

____

6 Ich kann meine Fahrkarte nicht finden. – Dann suche ich sie.

____

Spotlight on ...
Question tags

1 That's a great film, **isn't it?**
That's not a problem, **is it?**
- Frageanhängsel werden vor allem im mündlichen Englisch sehr häufig verwendet. Sie helfen, ein Gespräch flüssig zu halten, indem man z. B. Zustimmung sucht oder nachfragt. Im Deutschen würde man stattdessen „nicht (wahr)?“, „ja/gell?“ bzw. „oder?“ ans Ende des Satzes stellen.

2 Your sister has bought a new car, **hasn't she?**
- Bei einer positiven Aussage wird das Frageanhängsel verneint.

3 You can't drive a car, **can you?**
- Bei einer negativen Aussage wird das Frageanhängsel bejaht.

4 Your sister has bought a new car, **hasn't she?**
You like basketball, **don't you?**
- Wenn ein Hilfsverb (*have*, *be*, *can*, *will*) in der Frage steht, steht es auch im Frageanhängsel. Bei anderen Verben braucht man eine Form von *do*.

1 ***Complete the sentences with the right question tag. Use the negative form.***

1 Your grandparents live in Scotland, ______________ ?
2 You're a *Coldplay* fan, ______________ ?
3 You worked in a bakery, ______________ ?
4 Sarah can play the guitar, ______________ ?
5 You have a dog, ______________ ?
6 You've been to America, ______________ ?
7 There'll be a DJ at the party, ______________ ?
8 We need to leave soon, ______________ ?

2 ***Complete the sentences with the right question tag. Use the positive form.***

1 Mike doesn't eat meat, ______________ ?
2 You haven't seen Ben, ______________ ?
3 The Burtons don't live here, ______________ ?
4 Amy wasn't at the party, ______________ ?
5 You weren't very happy last night, ______________ ?
6 I haven't told you the news yet, ______________ ?
7 The weather wasn't very good, ______________ ?
8 She can't sing very well, ______________ ?

3 ***Match the parts to form question tags.***

1	You don't know my friend Linda,	a	does she?
2	You're going to be a teacher,	b	is it?
3	This colour is really nice,	c	hasn't he?
4	The house isn't theirs,	d	isn't it?
5	My mother told you about my problems,	e	didn't she?
6	You'll stop smoking,	f	aren't you?
7	Your father has moved again,	g	do you?
8	Sharon doesn't have a pet,	h	won't you?

4 ***Write the questions and add the right question tags.***

1 you be to London last year?
You went to London last year, didn't you?
2 you have a dog?
____
3 your little brother start school next year?
____
4 Faith not see the new film yet?
____
5 Steven not like football?
____
6 you can play the piano?
____
7 Debbie win the competition last week?
____
8 Carol have got a new car?
____

Simple past (► S. 22)

1 ***Fill in the table with the right simple past form of the following regular verbs.***

agree • apply • argue • belong • bury • die • enjoy • fit • grab

just -ed	-ied	without -e	double letter
		I agreed	

2 ***Complete the dialogue using the simple past.***

Jane — We ______ [1] (spend) our last holiday in the Netherlands.

Bob — That sounds nice. ______ [2] (you have) fun?

Jane — Oh yes, it ______ [3] (be) great. We ______ [4] (travel) around a bit and then we ______ [5] (visit) friends in Amsterdam.

Bob — Oh really? I ______ [6] (not know) you had friends there.

Jane — Yes, we ______ [7] (meet) them in England. They ______ [8] (work) there years ago.

Bob — Oh, I see. And ______ [9] (you like) Amsterdam?

Jane — It's a great city. Our friends ______ [10] (show) us all the sights.

Bob — Ah good. Somebody ______ [11] (tell) me they have some great museums there.

Jane — Yes, but we ______ [12] (not stay) long enough to visit them all!

Present perfect (► S. 24)

3 ***Tick [✓] the sentence which uses the right tense.***

1 **a** Last week I went to London by train. [ ]
  b Last week I've gone to London by train. [ ]

2 **a** I never saw so much snow before! [ ]
  b I've never seen so much snow before! [ ]

3 **a** My family moved here a hundred years ago or so. [ ]
  b My family has moved here a hundred years or so. [ ]

4 **a** Did you ever eat kangaroo meat? [ ]
  b Have you ever eaten kangaroo meat? [ ]

5 **a** Sally is ill. She didn't leave the house for two days. [ ]
  b Sally is ill. She hasn't left the house for two days. [ ]

6 **a** Great present! I wanted a red bag since I was a child. [ ]
  b Great present! I've wanted a red bag since I was a child. [ ]

7 **a** Did you see the new shop in town already? [ ]
  b Have you seen the new shop in town already? [ ]

8 **a** Mike didn't buy a new computer yet. [ ]
  b Mike hasn't bought a new computer yet. [ ]

4 ***Complete the sentences with the simple past or present perfect.***

1 Bill, ______ [1] (you call) Mr Collins today? – Sorry, I ______ [2] (not call) him yet. But I ______ [3] (speak) to his secretary this morning and he said he ______ [4] (be) in a meeting this afternoon.

2 ______ [5] (anybody see) the fax from Top Copy? I ______ [6] (give) it to Sarah yesterday and now it ______ [7] (disappear).

3 Sanita, I ______ [8] (just get) an email from Boswell & Co. They want to know if you ______ [9] (send) them their order last week.

Past progressive (▸ S. 27)

5 *Complete the email with the past progressive.*

New email

Send Chat Attach Addresses Fonts Save

Hi Sophie

It's 10 p.m. here in Australia – and 11 a.m. in England.

So while you ______________ [1] (sleep) last night, I ______________ [2] (work).

When I ______________ [3] (have) my lunch, I ______________ [4] (watch) the late news from England.

My phone ______________ [5] (ring) at 4 p.m. but I knew it couldn't be you because you ______________ [6] (still dream).

And when I ______________ [7] (eat) my evening meal, you ______________ [8] (probably have) breakfast.

So what ______________ [9] (you do) when I ______________ [10] (clean) my flat at 7 p.m.?

You ______________ [11] (probably get) ready for work – or ______________ [12] (you ride) your bike already?

Please write soon!

Lots of love, Pete

Past perfect (▸ S. 28)

6 *Which of the two actions took place first (1) and which later (2)? Write if the verb is in the simple past (s.p.) or in the past perfect (p.p.).*

1 We went for a walk [2] s.p.
after we had eaten. [1] p.p.

2 My brother phoned [ ] ______
when I had prepared everything for the party. [ ] ______

3 When I had gone on holiday, [ ] ______
somebody broke into my house. [ ] ______

4 I had just sat down on the sofa [ ] ______
when I heard the noise. [ ] ______

5 When I came into the room, [ ] ______
the others had already started talking. [ ] ______

6 After I had saved some money, [ ] ______
I bought a new TV. [ ] ______

7 *Cross out the wrong form.*

1 After I *had gone / went* on holiday, a postcard arrived.
2 We ran to the station, but the train *had gone / went*.
3 After I had worked all day, I *had gone / went* home.
4 Had you checked that everything was OK before you *had gone / went* for lunch?
5 We counted the money after the customers *had gone / went*.
6 Mike didn't hear the news because he *had gone / went* fishing.

8 *Complete the text with the past perfect form of the verbs in brackets.*

My partner ______________ [1] (be) on many safaris, so I wanted to go on one as well. After I ______________ [2] (book) the flight to Kenya, I got a bit frightened. Was this really such a good idea? But when I ______________ [3] (pack) my safari clothes, I felt better already. After the plane ______________ [4] (land) at Nairobi airport, I had lots of doubts [*Zweifel*] again. But the hotel was fine and two days later the safari started. I ______________ [5] (talk) to the tour guide before we climbed into the jeeps and he ______________ [6] (confirm) that we would have a great trip. But I ______________ [7] (not be) prepared for what I saw – I just ______________ [8] (not expect) to see so many wild animals. It was simply fantastic.

Future (► S. 30)

9 ***Write sentences using the will future.***

This is your future – listen carefully:

1 be / rich man / one day
You will be a rich man one day.

2 have / beautiful wife / two nice kids

____

3 your job / make / happy

____

4 many people / want to be / your friends

____

5 do sports regularly / always enjoy it

____

6 travel / all around the world

____

10 ***Look at the pictures and write sentences using the going to future and the verbs play or go.***

We're going to have a sporty weekend. Here are our plans:

1 [✔] Ella ______________________________ .

2 [✘] She ______________________________ .

3 [✔] Kira and Imran ______________________________ .

4 [✘] They ______________________________ .

5 [✔] I ______________________________ .

6 [✘] I ______________________________ .

11 ***Cross out the wrong future form.***

1 It's my birthday next week. I *will be / am being* 16.

2 Is that bag heavy? I *carry / will carry* it for you.

3 The bus *leaves / will leave* at 10 o'clock.

4 I *will work / am working* on Saturday.

5 Next month *I go / am going* to Austria.

6 Here's Andrew's present. Do you think he *will / is going to* like it?

Question tags (► S. 32)

12 ***An interview. Match the sentences with the right question tags.***

1	You've always wanted to be a star, … – Yes, I have.	a	isn't she?
2	You learned to sing very early, … – Yes, I did. I was five.	b	don't you?
3	But you still can't play the guitar, … – No, I can't. Pity!	c	won't you?
4	Well, your fans all like you very much, … – Yes, they do. And I like them!	d	haven't you?
5	Your manager is one of the best, … – Yes, she is. She's great.	e	can you?
6	You like being on tour, … – Yes, I do. It's so interesting.	f	aren't we kids?
7	So you will come to Wales again, … – Of course I will!	g	don't they?
8	Great! We're all looking forward to that, … – Thank you very much.	h	didn't you?

13 Modal verbs A

can · could · may · might

A General

1 He **can** swim.
I **may** come later.
They **might not** go at all.

- Die oben genannten modalen Hilfsverben verändern ihre Form nicht. Man verwendet sie meist mit der Grundform eines Verbs. Ihre Verneinung wird mit *not* gebildet.

2 **Could** you help me, please? – Yes, I **can**. / No, **I can't**.
What **can** I do for you?

- Um eine Frage zu bilden, stellt man Hilfsverb und Subjekt um. Das gilt auch für Fragen mit Fragewörtern.

B Ability *(Fähigkeit)*

1 He **can** swim. Babies **cannot/can't** walk.

- Um über eine Fähigkeit zu sprechen, benutzt man *can*. Die verneinte Form heißt *cannot* (Kurzform *can't*).

2 I **couldn't** find the way.
We **were able to** see the ocean from the window.
Will you **be able to** use your hand again?

- *could* (verneint *could not*; Kurzform *couldn't*) kann in manchen Fällen als Vergangenheitsform von *can* benutzt werden, vor allem, wenn eine Aussage verneint wird. Bei bejahten Sätzen wird stattdessen meist *be able to* + Grundform verwendet; ebenso als Zukunftsform.

C Permission *(Erlaubnis)*

May I use your mobile, please? – Yes, you **may**. / No, you **may not**.
Could we stay a bit longer, please? – Yes, you **can**. / No, you **can't**.
Yes, you **can** go to the party.
Will we **be allowed to** smoke there?

- Mit *may, could* und *can* bittet man um Erlaubnis, etwas zu tun, oder sagt, was jemand tun darf. *May* ist am höflichsten; auch *could* (hier: *könnte/n*) ist recht höflich. Oft gebraucht man jedoch einfach *can*. Nur mit *be allowed to* + Grundform kann man auch über Zukünftiges sprechen.

D Possibility *(Möglichkeit)*

I **may** have to leave soon.
Sue **might** learn Spanish next year.
He **could** be hungry.

- Mit *may, might* und *could* (= könnte/n) sagt man, was wahrscheinlich oder vielleicht der Fall ist. *Can* ist hier allerdings nicht möglich. Im Deutschen verwendet man in solchen Sätzen oft das Wort „vielleicht".

Cool careers

"I want to be a florist because I love flowers. I could give advice to customers who don't know much about flowers. I may even design flower decorations for weddings."

"My dream job is to be a bus driver because I love driving. I was able to drive at the age of 14 (of course I wasn't allowed to!). I know it's a stressful job, but I can deal *[umgehen]* with stress quite well. And I might even get a uniform – I'd like that."

"I'm going to be a travel agent *[Reisebürokauffrau/-mann]*. I'll be able to help people with their holiday plans. I can speak a little German and Spanish, as well as English, of course, so I could work in an international agency."

"I like working with wood, so I'd like to be a carpenter. Carpenters can work anywhere – in the building industry or in a small firm, for example. I could even start my own business."

1 ***Which phrases express an ability? Which phrases express a possibility? Write them down in the table.***

ability	possibility

2 ***Write questions about the teenagers' dream jobs.***

1 work / florists / can / where

____?

2 myself / for / can / as a / travel agent / I / work

____?

3 my / dog / I / will / able / to work / to take / be

____?

4 their / bus drivers / can / route / favourite / pick

____?

5 I / will / be / to bring / tools / my own / able

____?

6 able / I / to use / my French / be / will

____?

3 ***New at the job. Read the questions and complete the short answers.***

1 Could you help me with this booking, please?

Yes, ________________ .

2 May I make a private phone call, please?

Yes, ________________ .

3 Can I book this flight?

No, ________________ .

4 May I use your pen?

Yes, ________________ .

5 Can I take this home with me?

No, ________________ .

6 Can I change my route today?

Yes, ________________ !

4 ***Complete the text with the right words from the box.***

can • can't • couldn't • may not • might • was able to

I've always wanted to be a reporter. I ________________ [1] read and write when I was 4 years old. (My sisters still ________________ [2] read when they were 6!) Now I'm 15 and I ________________ [3] speak German and French, as well as English. (My sisters still ________________ [4] speak a foreign language!) I ________________ [5] go to Germany for a while when I've finished school. (My sisters still ________________ [6] leave the country – they don't have passports!) My parents said that they ________________ [7] give me some money. It ________________ [8] be enough, though. That's why I need a summer job.

5 ***Use the modal verbs can, could, may or might to rewrite the sentences about Mike's work experience.***
There might be several possibilities.

1 He isn't allowed to talk to customers.
He can't talk to customers.

2 It's possible that he will get a job there later.

____

3 He wasn't able to use the computer programme when he started.

____

4 He's allowed to answer some emails now.

____

5 He's able to understand what his colleagues are talking about now.

____

6 Perhaps he will book a trip for himself soon!

____

6 ***Use modal verbs to translate the following sentences.***
There might be several possibilities.

1 Kann ich Ihnen behilflich sein?

____

2 Ich kann dieses Werkzeug nicht benutzen.

____

3 Ich werde bald mein Geschäft eröffnen können.

____

4 Ich konnte dich nicht hören.

____

5 Könnten Sie das bitte wiederholen?

____

6 Dürfte ich ein Telefongespräch führen?

____

7 Tom darf heute früher gehen.

____

8 Niemand durfte das Büro verlassen.

____

9 Dürfen wir hier rauchen?

____

10 Paula lernt nächstes Jahr vielleicht Deutsch.

____

14 Modal verbs B

should · must · have to · need to · needn't

A General

1 We **must** pay this bill.
Shouldn't you go home now?

- *must* und *should* verändern ihre Form nicht. Man verwendet sie meist mit der Grundform eines Verbs. Ihre Verneinung wird mit *not* gebildet. Fragen werden durch die Änderung der Wortstellung gebildet.

2 Emma **has to** write an email to a customer.
Does Ben **need to** buy a new car?
You **needn't** worry.

- *have to* und *need to* gleichen Vollverben; für Verneinung und Fragestellung braucht man die Umschreibung mit *do*. Achtung: *need* wird oft *needn't* verneint und braucht dann kein *to* mehr!

B Obligation/Advice *(Verpflichtung/Ratschlag)*

I **should** phone my colleague.
You **shouldn't** work so much.

- Mit *should* drückt man eine Verpflichtung aus oder gibt jemandem einen Rat.

C Necessity *(Notwendigkeit)*

1 You **must** be friendly to the customers.
We **have to** wear a helmet.
Tom **needs to** be more careful.

- Um über eine Notwendigkeit oder einen Zwang zu sprechen, benutzt man *must*, *have to* oder *need to*.

2 Bill **doesn't have to** work longer.
You **needn't** phone him.

- Will man sagen, dass jemand etwas nicht machen muss, benutzt man *don't have to* oder *needn't*. *Mustn't* (nicht dürfen) ist hier nicht möglich.

3 Lucy **had to** wait for two hours.
Will you **have to** wear a uniform?

- Will man über vergangene oder zukünftige Notwendigkeiten sprechen, benutzt man meist die entsprechende Form von *have to*.

Watch out!

mustn't heißt niemals „nicht müssen": *You* ***mustn't*** *be late.* = Du **darfst nicht** zu spät kommen.

On the job tips

1 ***Look at the tips for young people who are just starting work and cross out the wrong form.***

You *should / shouldn't*[1] make a good impression [*Eindruck*] on your first day at work. Here are some tips:

- You *should / shouldn't*[2] get things ready for your first day the night before.
- You *should / shouldn't*[3] forget to check the timetables [*Fahrpläne*] if you use buses or trains.
- You *should / shouldn't*[4] get up early enough because you don't know yet how much time you'll need.
- You *should / shouldn't*[5] be late!
- At work you *should / shouldn't*[6] be polite to everybody as you don't know who might be able to help you later.
- You *should / shouldn't*[7] find out about the rules of your workplace, the official and the unofficial ones.
- You *should / shouldn't*[8] ask lots of questions and try to remember the answers.

2 ***Mick's first day at work. Complete the sentences with a form of (not) have to.***

1 Mick ______________ get up early to be at work on time this morning.
2 ______________ wait long for the train?
3 He ______________ pay a lot for the ticket though because he has a railcard.
4 He now ______________ take the train every day.
5 Mick ______________ buy a car if there are problems with getting to work on the train.

3 ***Mick has had his first day at work. Complete his thoughts with mustn't or don't have to.***

1 I ______________ be late.
2 I ______________ check the train timetable anymore.
3 I ______________ get up as early as today anymore.
4 I ______________ forget my new colleagues' names.
5 I really like my new job. I ______________ lose it.
6 I now know that I ______________ to take my lunch with me – the food in the canteen is really good!

4 ***Jack works in an office and Ella is a shop assistant. Use modal verbs to write the opposite sentences for Jack.***
There is sometimes more than one possibility.

1 Ella needs to look as good as possible.
Jack doesn't have to look as good as possible.

2 Ella has to talk to customers a lot.
_______________ to customers a lot.

3 She must always smile.
_______________ smile.

4 Ella must work on Saturdays and some Sundays.
_______________ on Saturdays and some Sundays.

5 She needn't work on Mondays though.
_______________ on Mondays though.

6 Ella has to work till 10 p.m. sometimes.
_______________ till 10 p.m. sometimes.

7 She needn't use a computer at work.
_______________ a computer at work.

8 She will have to go on a training course soon.
_______________ on a training course soon.

5 ***Match the sentence halves.***

1 Jim's boss says he needs [ ]
2 This job will have to [ ]
3 You must [ ]
4 I needn't [ ]
5 Phil didn't have to [ ]
6 My boss says I should be [ ]
7 Pat doesn't have [ ]
8 Sue always had to [ ]

a write the email because his boss did it instead.
b to make more money.
c eat alone last year. Now she has found a friend.
d have worried. It was all OK.
e to stay any longer.
f change your attitude [*Haltung*] now.
g more careful in future.
h be finished by next weekend.

6 ***Bullying at work – what can you do? Complete the sentences with the right modal.***

1 You _______________ (*nicht müssen*) live with bullying at work.

2 The most important rule is: If you feel bullied, you _______________ (*müssen*) tell the person to stop.

3 The person _______________ (*nicht dürfen*) stay quiet and not talk about the problem.

4 You _______________ (*sollen*) keep a diary of events, so you won't forget any details.

5 If the bullying doesn't stop, you _______________ (*müssen*) tell somebody about it.

6 Remember: You _______________ (*nicht müssen*) deal with this alone.

7 ***Polite conversation at work. Pick the right modal and cross out the wrong one.***

1 *Must / May* I ask you a question, please?
2 *Could / Shouldn't* you show me the way to the fax machine, please?
3 *Mustn't / Should* I use this paper for the printer?
4 *Do I have to / Might I* press this button or that one?
5 The green light *could / has to* be on, right?
6 Excuse me, but I really *must / can* phone this customer before lunch.
7 You *needn't / mustn't* show me how to use the phone, thank you.
8 I know I *shouldn't / needn't* ask, but perhaps you can tell me where I can buy some chocolate?
9 I *might / must* have to leave earlier tomorrow. Is that OK?
10 *Can I / Do I have to* phone my mother quickly?
11 I *need to / shouldn't* tell her that I'll be late.

15 Gerund

1 **Swimming** is my hobby.
I enjoy **cycling** too.
Ron is good at **playing** basketball.

- Mit dem Gerundium kann man über Tätigkeiten sprechen. Es wird meist wie ein Nomen gebraucht: *Schwimmen ist mein Hobby.*

2 Ru**nn**ing is great to keep fit.
Layla is tired of ri**d**ing her bike all the time.

- Das Gerundium entspricht der *-ing*-Form des Verbs. Dabei werden Infinitivendungen wie *-m*, *-n* oder *-t* nach kurz gesprochenen Silben verdoppelt (z.B. *swim, begin, run, get, put*); ein stummes *-e* am Ende des Infinitivs (z.B. *drive, make, ride, use*) fällt weg.

3 **Sailing** is my favourite activity.

- Das Gerundium kann Subjekt eines Satzes sein.

4 I like **watching** sports.
Tom stopped **smoking** last year.

- Das Gerundium kann Objekt eines Satzes sein. Dabei steht es häufig nach Verben des Anfangens oder Aufhörens (*begin/start, finish/stop/give up*) und immer nach folgenden Verben: *enjoy, finish, give up, imagine, keep, mention, miss, practise, recommend, risk, suggest.*

5 I'm worried about **running** in the race [*Rennen*] tomorrow.

- Folgt ein Verb auf eine Präposition, steht es als Gerundium. Häufige Ausdrücke mit Präpositionen sind z.B. *angry/sorry/worried about, afraid/tired of, depend on, fed up with, good/bad at, interested in, think of.*

Watch out!

Bei diesen Ausdrücken folgt auf das *to* kein Infinitiv, sondern ein Gerundium:
*I'm looking forward **to meeting** you.*
[Ich freue mich darauf, Sie kennenzulernen.]
*I'm used **to walking** long distances.*
[Ich bin daran gewöhnt, lange Strecken zu gehen.]

Fair sports?

1a ***Look at the pictures and make the gerunds. Put them in the crossword.***

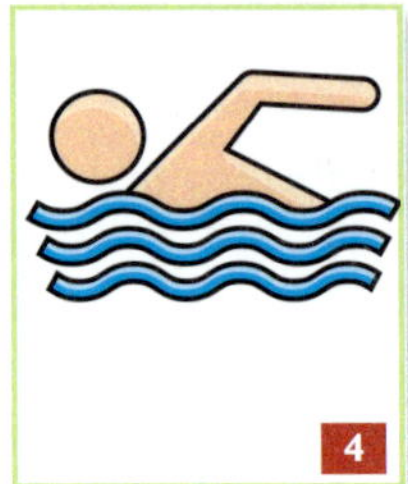

1b ***Now put the gerunds from above in these sentences.***

1 Mike is very interested in ____________________ . He has a mountain bike now.

2 He's a bit tired of ____________________ . He thinks races are boring.

3 I love water. ____________________ is my favourite activity. I'm going to join a team soon.

4 But I don't like ____________________ into the water very much. I often hurt myself.

5 Sue is really good at ____________________ . She has no problem with heights.

6 She isn't bad at ____________________ either, but of course you need snow for that.

1c ***Look at the sentences in 1b again. Decide which sentences are examples of the following structures:***

1 Gerund as subject: Sentence(s) no. ______

2 Gerund as object: Sentence(s) no. ______

3 Gerund after phrase + preposition: Sentence(s) no. ______

2 ***Rewrite these sentences using the gerund.***

1 The baseball player misses ~~to have~~ fun.

____

2 The dancer enjoys ~~to look~~ good.

____

3 The tennis player keeps ~~to think~~ about losing.

____

4 He imagines ~~to be~~ the best runner in the world.

____

5 The football player mentions ~~to stay~~ healthy.

____

3a ***Read the story and put in the gerunds.***

Suzi and Layla both enjoyed ______________ 1 *(Laufen)* very much. They often trained together. Suzi was much better at ______________ 2 *(Laufen)* than Layla. She was really fast. Her trainer said she could be part of the team soon . ______________ 3 *(Gewinnen)* the next race was very important for that. Suzi told Layla that she was really worried about ______________ 4 *(Verlieren)*. She said that she was thinking about ______________ 5 *(Suchen)* for help on the internet. Layla didn't know what she meant and said nothing. On the day of the race they went for lunch together, but Suzi didn't eat anything. " ______________ 6 *(Essen)* is so important," Layla said, but Suzi said that she felt really fit and was really looking forward to ______________ 7 *(Laufen)* now. When Layla asked what had changed, Suzi smiled and said that was her secret. Layla started ______________ 8 *(sich Sorgen machen)*. Had Suzi taken drugs?

3b ***Now write down all the phrase + preposition gerunds from the story.***

1 ______________________________

2 ______________________________

3 ______________________________

4 ______________________________

4 ***Rewrite these sentences using the gerund.***

1 The trainer said, 'Let's try some tablets.'

The trainer suggested *trying some tablets*.

2 Suzi said, 'I took some drugs before the race.'

Suzi admitted ______________________________ .

3 Rob said, 'I saw Lucy after the race.'

Rob mentioned ______________________________ .

4 My mum said, 'You should buy some new running shoes.'

My mum recommended ______________________________ .

5 Rachel said, 'I don't take drugs anymore.'

Rachel has stopped ______________________________ .

5 ***Would they take drugs? Complete the sentences with a prepositon from the box and a gerund.***

about • at • in • of • to • with

1 Winning would be great, but Jack and Jill are mainly interested ______________ (have fun).

2 I couldn't do it. I'm just not very good ______________ (lie).

3 Paul is afraid ______________ (get) ill. He wants to stay fit and healthy.

4 Carl is so worried ______________ (lose). He thinks he could probably get away with it.

5 Alice is fed up ______________ (be) last. Her trainer said he could give her some 'healthy tablets'.

6 My friends are used ______________ (take) tablets. They've taken them before races for years.

Contrast: Gerund ►◄ infinitive

1 I **keep having** the same dream.
He's good **at dancing**.
Das Gerundium folgt immer auf bestimmte Verben, z.B. *enjoy, finish, give up, imagine, keep, mention, miss, practise, recommend, risk, suggest*. Nach einer Präposition steht das Verb ebenfalls als Gerundium, z.B. nach *angry/sorry/worried about, afraid/tired of, depend on, fed up with, good/bad at, interested in, think of*.

2 You **promised to** wash the car!
Auf einige Verben folgt immer der Infinitiv, z.B. auf *afford, agree, decide, expect, hope, learn, manage, offer, plan, promise, seem, want, wish*.

3 I **love playing** basketball.
I **love to play** basketball.
I **would love to play** basketball.
Auf einige Verben kann sowohl das Gerundium als auch der Infinitiv folgen, z. B. auf *begin/start, hate, like, love*. Auf *would hate/like/love* folgt allerdings immer der Infinitiv.

4 *Tim stopped* ***talking*** *when Pat arrived.* (= hörte auf zu reden) ►◄ *Tim stopped* ***to talk*** *with Pat.* (= hielt an, um zu reden)

Manche Verben ändern ihre Bedeutung, je nachdem, ob sie mit einem Gerundium oder einem Infinitiv verbunden werden. Weitere Beispiele: *forget doing something* (= vergessen, das man etwas getan hat) – *forget to do something* (vergessen, etwas zu tun); *remember doing something* (= sich daran erinnern, dass man etwas getan hat) – *remember to do sth* (= daran denken, etwas zu tun).

1 ***Cross out the wrong forms where necessary.***
Careful: Sometimes both forms are possible.

1 I'm sorry about *being / to be* late.
2 I hate *doing / to do* housework when the weather is good.
3 Mike offered *going / to go* shopping later.
4 Tim is really interested *in sailing / to sail*.
5 Imagine *having / to have* a holiday now!
6 In the summer Sophie always misses *skiing / to ski*.
7 We've started *learning / to learn* French for the holiday.
8 I stopped *playing / to play* computer games when my father came home.
9 Do you plan *visiting / to visit* Rome when you're in Italy?
10 Please remember *taking / to take* the letter to the post office.

2 ***Tick [✔] the correct translation.***
Careful: Sometimes both forms are possible.

1 *Ich habe aufgehört, zu rauchen.*
[ ] a) I stopped smoking.
[ ] b) I stopped to smoke.

2 *Ich habe angefangen, das Buch zu lesen.*
[ ] a) I started reading the book.
[ ] b) I started to read the book.

3 *Ich erinnere mich daran, dass ich es ihm gesagt habe.*
[ ] a) I remember telling him.
[ ] b) I remember to tell him.

4 *Ich spiele sehr gern Tischtennis.*
[ ] a) I like playing table tennis.
[ ] b) I like to play table tennis.

5 *Ich habe vergessen, meine Mutter anzurufen.*
[ ] a) I forgot calling my mother.
[ ] b) I forgot to call my mother.

6 *Bitte denke daran, das Licht auszuschalten.*
[ ] a) Please remember to turn off the light.
[ ] b) Please remember turning off the light.

3 ***Complete these sentences and questions. Use the right form of the verb and the gerund or the infinitive.***

1 Do ______________ (want buy) yourself a new mobile?
2 Mum ______________ (tired of listen) to your stories.
3 I ______________ (not remember see) you at the party.
4 Did Tina ______________ (enjoy cook) last night?
5 I ______________ (suggest watch) a DVD later.
6 My sister ______________ (love play) football.
7 Rosie ______________ (fed up with have) so little money.
8 I couldn't ______________ (stop laugh). It was so funny.

Spotlight on ...
Participles

1 a) I love **riding** my bike.
b) The girls **were having** fun.

- a) Das *present participle* hat dieselbe Form wie das Gerundium, Vergleich Seite 40. b) Mit dem *present participle* und einer Form von *be* werden alle Verlaufsformen (*progressive forms*) gebildet.

2 a) The train **has** just **arrived**.
b) The cake **was made** by Fatima.

- a) Mit dem *past participle* und einer Form von *have* werden die Perfektformen (*present/past perfect*) gebildet, Vergleich Seite 24. b) Mit dem *past participle* und einer Form von *be* bildet man das Passiv.

3 A **dancing** bear? What a nice present!
Look at all those people **waiting**.
Tim is in hospital with a **broken** leg.

- Das *participle* kann (wie ein Adjektiv) dazu benutzt werden, nähere Informationen über ein Nomen zu geben. *Present participles* können vor oder nach einem Nomen stehen.

4 The woman who is sitting over there seems nice.
The woman **sitting** over there seems nice.
'Beat it' is a song which was sung by Michael Jackson.
'Beat it' is a song **sung** by Michael Jackson.

- Man kann ein *participle* benutzen, um einen Relativsatz zu kürzen, indem man *which/who* und die Form von *be* weglässt.

1 ***Underline the participle in each sentence and tick [✔] whether it is a present or a past participle.***

1 I couldn't get past the people dancing.
[ ] present [ ] past

2 Does your family often buy frozen food?
[ ] present [ ] past

3 The teacher tried to talk to the screaming children.
[ ] present [ ] past

4 The shocked workers quickly tried to get help.
[ ] present [ ] past

5 I looked after the crying baby.
[ ] present [ ] past

6 The worried parents phoned the teachers every day.
[ ] present [ ] past

2 ***Complete the sentences with the present or past participle of the verbs in the box.***

close • lose • play • sleep • steal • wait

1 (present participle) Psst! Don't wake the ______________ dog.

2 (past participle) Have they found that ______________ girl yet?

3 (past participle) I can't see through ______________ doors!

4 (past participle) The police looked everywhere for the ______________ computers.

5 (present participle) The teacher spoke to the ______________ students.

6 (present participle) We mustn't disturb the children ______________ .

3 ***Use a participle to shorten these sentences.***

1 The man who is dancing with my sister comes from Canada.

____

2 The shop which is opening on the High Street today sells sweets.

____

3 That's the skirt that was designed by Karl Lagerfeld.

____

4 Look at all the people who are standing in line at the baker's.

____

5 The number of car accidents which are caused by alcohol is rising.

____

6 That's the dress I want, the one which is hanging in the window.

____

16 Adjectives

1 Jess is a **beautiful** girl.
That's a really **nice** T-shirt.
I'm quite **tired**.

- Adjektive (Eigenschaftswörter) geben Auskunft über eine Sache oder eine Person. Man kann sie mit Wörtern wie *very, really* oder *too* verstärken oder mit *quite* einschränken.

2 This is my **new** boyfriend.
He looks **friendly**.
Gordon is **fantastic**!

- Adjektive stehen oft direkt vor einem Nomen oder Pronomen. Sie können auch nach den folgenden Verben stehen: *appear, be, become, get, feel, look, seem, smell, sound, taste.*

3 Your dog is very **unfriendly**.
It's an **indirect** way.

- Durch das Hinzufügen der Vorsilben *un-* oder *in-* wird der Gegensatz mancher Adjektive gebildet. Ausnahmen: *il-* vor Adjektiven, die mit *l* beginnen (*legal – illegal*) und *im-* vor Adjektiven, die mit *p* beginnen (*perfect – imperfect*).

Comparison

1 Bill is **as** old **as** Sarah.
The film isn't **as** good **as** the book.

- Mit *(not) as … as* (= (nicht) so … wie) kann man Vergleiche anstellen.

2 I'm **older than** Sue. Anne is **the oldest** here.
busy – busi**er** – busi**est**
nice – nice**r** – nice**st**
big – big**ger** – big**gest**

- Einsilbige Adjektive sowie zweisilbige Adjektive, die auf *-y* enden, werden mit *-er (comparative form)* bzw. *-est (superlative form)* gesteigert. Aufgepasst: ein *-y* wird zu *-i*, ein stummes *-e* am Ende fällt weg und Endungen wie *-g*, *-n* oder *-t* werden nach kurz gesprochenen Silben oft verdoppelt.
- This dress is **more expensive than** that one.
In fact, it's **the most expensive** dress in the shop.
famous – **more** famous – **most** famous
modern – **more** modern – **most** modern
- Alle drei- und mehrsilbigen sowie einige zweisilbige Adjektive werden durch Hinzufügen von *more* bzw. *most* vor dem Adjektiv gesteigert.

3 good – **better** – **best**
bad – **worse** – **worst**

- Beachte die Sonderformen.

Watch out!

Sue is younger than **me**. *NOT* ~~*Sue is younger than I*~~.

Perfect!?

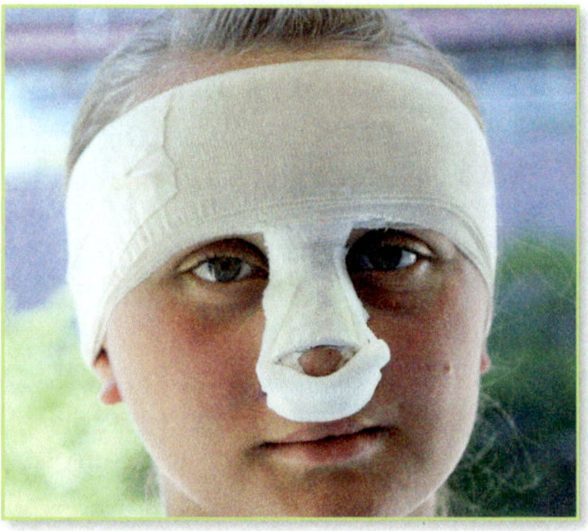

Plastic surgery *[Schönheitsoperationen]*

Samira's story: "I was 17 and everything seemed perfect about me, except my nose. I had a nice body, nice personality, but I was so unattractive because I had a big nose! I decided to get plastic surgery. It was the most painful experience of my life! I remember waking up with terrible pain. But today I have a normal nose. Nobody has ever commented on it though. Would I do it again? No, I wouldn't. It's just not important enough."

Helen's story: "I decided to have my nose done because I've always had breathing problems [*Atemprobleme*]. And I wanted to look better – I didn't like that small bump [*Höcker*] on my nose. After the surgery, things weren't easy. There were moments when the pain was so horrible that I wished I hadn't had the surgery … Today I can breathe through my nose and I love my new face. My friends think that I look the same. But when I see myself in the mirror, I see a perfect face. Would I do it again? Yes, definitely. I feel so much better now."

1a ***Underline all the adjectives in Samira's (10) and Helen's (8) story.***

1b ***Now compare the two stories. Circle the correct form: than or as.***

1 Samira felt more unattractive *than / as* Helen.
2 Looking better wasn't quite as important for Helen *than / as* for Samira.
3 Helen had more serious reasons for the surgery *than / as* Samira.
4 The pain was as terrible for Samira *than / as* it was for Helen.
5 The results of the surgery are more unimportant for Samira *than / as* for Helen.
6 Her new nose doesn't make Samira quite as happy *than / as* it does Helen.

2 ***Complete Josh's story with the opposite of the adjectives in brackets. Use one of these prefixes: il-, im-, in- or un-.***

I'm unhappy because I'm fat, really fat, and I feel very ____________ [1] (comfortable) with that. People can be quite ____________ [2] (tolerant) of fat people and they are often ____________ [3] (polite). That's why I try to stay at home as much as possible. I feel ____________ [4] (safe) anywhere else. I'm not sure, but sometimes I think it's because I'm fat that I'm still ____________ [5] (employed). But that's ____________ [6] (fair) because I'm a really good worker. It's also ____________ [7] (legal), but of course I can't prove [*beweisen*] that I haven't got a job because I'm fat. Perhaps I will get plastic surgery one day…

3 ***Which of the adjectives in the box take an -er in the comparative and an -est in the superlative form? Write them down in all three forms.***

angry • big • bored • boring • easy • excited • hot • interesting • polite • safe • surprising • thin • worried

1 *angry* ____ *angrier* ____ *angriest* ____
2 ____ ____ ____
3 ____ ____ ____
4 ____ ____ ____
5 ____ ____ ____
6 ____ ____ ____

4 ***Mirror, mirror, on the wall … Complete these sentences with the comparative or superlative forms of the adjectives in brackets.***

Your mirror can be one of the ____________ [1] (powerful) [*mächtig, einflussreich*] objects that you use. Can't stand looking in it in the mornings? Time for some advice! Don't hate your mirror – it can be ____________ [2] (friendly) than you think! Concentrating on what you don't like in the mirror is the ____________ [3] (bad) thing you can do. Instead, find the ____________ [4] (good) thing about yourself – and smile! You will feel much ____________ [5] (happy) than before.

5 ***Complete the sentences with the right adjective from the box in the comparative or superlative form.***

big • fat • good • worried • ugly

1 My friend Joe is quite thin. But he thinks he's the ____________ boy in town.
2 Laura thinks her nose is ____________ than my nose. But to me it seems quite small.
3 I think my girlfriend is very good-looking. But she thinks that she's the ____________ girl in the whole school.
4 Pete is ____________ about his looks than anybody else I know. But he looks great – he shouldn't worry.
5 Angie doesn't like her hair. But I think it's much ____________ than my hair.

6 ***Write sentences using the comparative or superlative form of the adjectives.***

1 I'm the / perfect / woman in the world
____
2 I'm / thin / than all the other women
____
3 I've got the / long / legs you've ever seen
____
4 My name is the / beautiful / name you've ever heard: Barbie!
____

7 ***Spot the mistake and correct the sentences. One sentence is already correct.***

1 My sister is beautifuler than me.
____
2 I think plastic surgery for teenagers should be unlegal.
____
3 Jason went to the most expensive doctor for his operation.
____
4 Laura is the tallest but I am taller as Jane.
____
5 Sarah is the most short person in the class.
____

17 Adverbs

1 The boys sing **beautifully**.
She drove her car **dangerously**.

- Adverbien der Art und Weise geben Auskunft darüber, auf welche Art und Weise etwas geschieht. Sie geben ergänzende Informationen über das Verb. Diese Adverbien stehen oft hinter dem Verb oder hinter dem Objekt des Verbs (aber **nie** zwischen Verb und Objekt!).

2 I waited **nervously**.
The door opens **easily**.
She dances **terribly**.

- In der Regel werden Adverbien durch Anhängen von *-ly* an ein Adjektiv gebildet. Die Adjektivendung *-y* wird im Adverb zu *-i-*; enden Adjektive z.B. auf *-ble*, wird im Adverb daraus *-bly*.

3 He ran **fast**.
She swims **well**.

- Einige Adverbien haben dieselbe Form wie das Adjektiv und brauchen keine *-ly*-Endung, z.B. *early/late, fast, hard, long, right/wrong*. Das Adverb zum Adjektiv *good* lautet *well*.

4 He became **angry**.

- Auf den folgenden Verben folgt ein Adjektiv statt eines Adverbs: *appear, be, become, feel, get, look, seem, smell, sound, taste*.

Comparison

1 Finn speaks German **as well as** Selina.

- Mit *(not) as* ... *as* (= (nicht) so ... wie) kann man Vergleiche anstellen.

2 Come here. You can sit **more comfortably** in this chair.
Of all the workers, Gavin works **most slowly**.

- In der Regel werden mit *-ly* gebildete Adverbien durch Hinzufügen von *more* bzw. *most* gesteigert.

3 I ran **faster than** all the others.

- Die Adverbien, die mit Adjektiven identisch sind, werden mit *-er (comparative form)* bzw. *-est (superlative form)* gesteigert.

4 **well – better – best**
badly – worse – worst

- Beachte die Sonderformen.

Modern travel

1 ***Make adverbs from the following adjectives.***
Careful: You can't always just put -ly at the end!

1 hard; 2 clear; 3 long; 4 wrong; 5 safe; 6 angry; 7 slow; 8 loud; 9 easy; 10 good; 11 bad

1	2	3	4	5	6	7	8	9	10	11
D	A	N	G	E	R	O	U	S	L	Y

2 ***Circle the star which marks where the adverb belongs in each sentence.***

Some people go to a travel agency [*Reisebüro*] to book their holidays. Why?

1 (well) The people there * know the market *.

2 (carefully) A travel agent explains * things to you *.

3 (more quickly) A travel agent can book * flights and hotel rooms * than you.

4 (more cheaply) A travel agent may * sell you your trip *.

Some people book their holidays on the internet. Why?

5 (comfortably) The customer can * stay at home *.

6 (carefully) The customer can * think about every detail *.

7 (freely) The customer * can choose *.

8 (more cheaply) The customer may * travel *.

3 *Complete the text with the right adverb form of the adjectives in brackets.*

Travel ___________ [1] **(cheap) – fly INAIR!**

We'll take you ___________ [2] (safe) to your destination [*Ziel*] anywhere in Europe. You can book all our flights ___________ [3] (easy) on the internet.

Step 1: Put in your flight dates and read the results ___________ [4] (careful).

Step 2: Choose your flight.

Step 3: Read your booking details ___________ [5] (slow) and check that everything is correct.

Step 4: You can now pay more ___________ [6] (simple) than ever – just put in your credit card details.

And that's it! Your flight is booked and we look forward to welcoming you on our flight soon.

4 *Getting ready. Find the adjective in the first sentence and underline it. Then complete the second sentence with the missing adverbs.*

1 Jeremy was happy. He sang ___________ while he was packing.

2 Emma was very excited. "Only two more days!" she shouted ___________ .

3 Their dog Max, a black poodle, had a loud voice. He started to bark ___________ .

4 They had found the perfect person to care for him. They knew that Emma's sister would look after him ___________ .

5 Jeremy laughed when he saw how bad Emma's bag looked. "You've packed it so ___________ !" he said.

6 Emma looked at Jeremy's bag. It looked good. "OK, you've packed yours ___________," she said. "Now you can do mine!"

5 *Adjective or adverb? Write the sentences.*

1 The motorway / be / very busy

____

2 However Jeremy and Emma / arrive / at the airport / early

____

3 They / go / to a coffee bar / quick / for a sandwich

____

4 Jeremy / buy / a cheap / map of Berlin

____

5 Suddenly it / be / rather / late / and they / wait / nervous / to get on the plane

____

6 They / find / their seats on the plane / easy

____

6 *In Berlin. Complete the sentences with the correct comparative adverb form of the adjectives in brackets.*

1 "Let's take the train. It goes much ___________ (fast) than the bus."

2 "Look, you can buy clothes ___________ (cheap) here than in London."

3 "I can't talk ___________ (long), Mum. It costs too much."

4 "Jeremy, I'm so tired. Can't we go to bed a little ___________ (early)?"

5 – "Oh Emma! Why can't you walk ___________ (quick)?!"

7 *Adjective or adverb? Cross out the wrong form.*
Remember: Not every verb is followed by an adverb!

1 The music sounded *loud / loudly*. The people sang *loud / loudly*.

2 They ate *good / well* in Berlin. The food tasted *good / well*.

3 The dog felt *soft / softly*. Emma's sister stroked [*streichelte*] it *soft / softly*.

4 The tour guide looked *nice / nicely* and he spoke *nice / nicely* to Emma and Jeremy.

5 The bus seemed *bad / badly*. It was driven *bad / badly* too.

6 Emma and Jeremy were *happy / happily*. They flew home *happy / happily*.

Test 3

Modal verbs A (▸ S. 36)

1 ***Write sentences using the right form of can or be able to.***

1 I / not / find keys / this morning

____

2 Adam / not / leave school / next year

____

3 My sister / go surfing / last summer

____

4 I / not / play the piano but I / play the guitar

____

5 Linda / not / come to London / tomorrow

____

6 My parents / not / phone me / two days ago

____

2 ***Complete the questions using the right modal verb.***

1 ______________ borrow your bike for an hour?

– Yes, you may.

2 ______________ go on holiday with you?

– No, he couldn't.

3 ______________ go out with Anna tonight?

– Yes, she can.

4 ______________ be allowed to dance at the party?

– Yes, we will.

5 ______________ smoke here?

– No, they can't.

6 ______________ help me later?

– Yes, I can.

Modal verbs B (▸ S. 38)

3 ***Cross out the wrong modal form.***

1 I *should / may* have to work at the weekend.

2 What's the matter with the dog?

– I don't know. He *could / mustn't* be tired.

3 Let's phone Lucy. She *can / might* know the answer.

4 I *mustn't / don't have to* lose these keys.

5 You *mustn't / needn't* do that now. We can do it together later.

4 ***The modal phrase in each sentence is wrong. Correct the sentences using one of the modals in the box below.***
Sometimes there is more than one possibility.

have to • needn't • should • shouldn't

1 John mustn't wear a suit at work because he works in a bank.

____

2 You must count all the apples. Just weigh them.

____

3 Ray, you can work every weekend. You really need a break.

____

4 Mustn't I talk to my boss about the bullying?

____

5 Must you travel a lot in your new job?

____

5 ***Complete these rules for dog owners with modal forms.***
Sometimes there is more than one possibility.

1 You ______________ feed your dog regularly.

2 You ______________ feed a dog twice a day – once is enough.

3 You ______________ worry when the dog barks. That's quite normal.

4 The dog ______________ be outside all day. Two hours a day are enough.

5 You ______________ play with a young dog very often.

6 You ______________ very careful when there are small children around.

Gerund (▸ S. 40)

6 ***Rewrite the sentences using the same verb. Put the gerund at the beginning of the sentences.***

1 It's great fun to hike.

Hiking is great fun.

2 It's my hobby to collect comics.

____

3 It's great to play beach volleyball in the summer.

____

4 It's not enough to dream about a good job.

____

5 It's part of my job to check the machines.

____

6 It isn't easy to write a daily blog.

____

7 It is difficult to ride a horse.

____

8 It's boring to read books.

____

7 ***Write the answers to these questions.***

1 Why do you want to be a florist? – (interested in / sell / flowers)

Because I'm interested in selling flowers.

2 Why do you want to go home? – (fed up with / play / basketball)

____

3 Why don't you want to play football? – (worried about / hurt / my leg)

____

4 Why do you want to borrow my car? – (think of / go / into town)

____

5 Why do you want to work as a teacher? – (good at / talk to / kids)

____

6 Why do you want to play a new sport? – (tired of / play / ice hockey / all the time)

____

8 ***Gerund, infinitive or both? Tick [✓] the right option(s).***

1	I miss cooking	✓	I miss to cook	
2	I expect arriving		I expect to arrive	
3	she hates dancing		she hates to dance	
4	they start smoking		they start to smoke	
5	I promise coming		I promise to come	
6	she seems dreaming		she seems to dream	
7	you like drawing		you like to draw	
8	I want going		I want to go	
9	he keeps talking		he keeps to talk	
10	she agrees helping		she agrees to help	

9 ***Complete the sentences with a gerund, an infinitive or both.***

1 Never be late. You can't risk ________________ (lose) your job.

2 After about an hour, the machine began ________________ (make) a funny noise.

3 I hope ________________ (start) a new job next week.

4 We went to the coast last summer. I really enjoyed ________________ (swim) in the sea.

5 Louise misses ________________ (go out) with her friends at home.

6 I'm not very good at ________________ (play) basketball.

7 I've decided ________________ (move) to Australia.

8 I really like ________________ (listen) to her play the piano.

Participles (▸ S. 43)

10 ***Complete the sentences with a present or past participle of the verbs in the box.***

break • change • choose • copy • sit • stop

1 The ________________ climate isn't a new problem.

2 You aren't allowed to sell ________________ DVDs.

3 The policeman walked over to the ________________ car.

4 That's my dog ________________ over there.

5 Can you repair my ________________ radio, please?

6 The ________________ students became group leaders.

Adjectives (► S. 44)

11 ***Make comparisons.***

+ better/… than, – not better/… than
= as good/… as, ≠ not as good/… as

1 Mike / + fast / Andy
Mike is faster than Andy.

2 Oslo / + cold / Madrid

____

3 Cindy / – tall / Alice

____

4 fruit / + healthy / chocolate

____

5 the new film / ≠ romantic / the old film

____

6 my mother / = nervous / my father

____

7 my sister / + young / me

____

8 comics / – popular / youth magazines

____

12 ***Complete the sentences with the superlative form of the adjectives in brackets.***

1 I think Britney Spears is ______________ (good) singer in the world!

2 The last Harry Potter book was ______________ (exciting) one.

3 This coat here is ______________ (cheap).

4 Sarah is ______________ (important) person in the company.

5 The exam yesterday was ______________ (difficult) exam I've ever done!

6 This is ______________ (bad) song ever!

Adverbs (► S. 46)

13 ***Complete the sentences with the right adverb.***

1 At the beginning of the interview, Helen laughed ______________ (nervous).

2 My sister speaks French very ______________ (good).

3 Mark went skiing and hurt himself ______________ (bad).

4 You can create a new website ______________ (easy) with our new software.

5 Paul has to work ______________ (fast) in his new job.

6 My brother cooks ______________ (wonderful).

14 ***Adverb or adjective? Complete the sentences with the correct form of the verbs in the box.***

bad • nervous • wrong

1 Tina smoked ______________ .

2 Did you hear about Bill's accident? It sounds ______________ .

3 This can't work. It looks ______________ .

4 I'm getting more and more ______________ about the exams.

5 I didn't train enough, so I ran ______________ .

6 All the clocks in the house went ______________ .

15 ***Write the sentences.***

Tom is always better than Tim.

1 (ride bike / fast)
Tom rides his bike faster than Tim.

2 (jog / long)

______________________________ .

3 (sing / beautiful)

______________________________ .

4 (play football / good)

______________________________ .

5 (shout / loud)

______________________________ .

6 (be / friendly)

______________________________ .

He's perfect!

18 Relative clauses

1 Mr Smith is the man **who/that** works at the post office.
I bought the car **which/that** we looked at last week.

- Relativsätze geben zusätzliche Informationen über eine Person oder einen Gegenstand. Sie werden mit *who* (nur für Personen) oder *which* (für Gegenstände oder Tiere) eingeleitet; *that* kann aber sowohl anstelle von *who* als auch anstelle von *which* stehen.

2 Lou works in a shop which sells clothes.
= Lou works in a shop. The shop sells clothes.
The man who helped you last week is my neighbour.
= The man helped you last week. He is my neighbour.

- Durch einen Relativsatz kann man zwei einfache Sätze miteinander verbinden. Der Relativsatz kann auch mitten im Satz stehen.

3 This is the T-shirt ~~that~~ I bought.
The girl ~~who~~ I like is called Emily.

- Ist das Relativpronomen Objekt, sind englische Relativsätze auch ohne *who/that* verständlich.

4 The woman ~~who is~~ serving us is my cousin.
The dog ~~that was~~ running through your garden belonged to me.

- In Relativsätzen mit Verlaufsform (*be* + *-ing*) können sowohl *who/that* als auch die Form von *be* weggelassen werden (Vergleich S. 43).

Watch out!

Englischen Relativsätze, die genauere Informationen über eine Person oder einen Gegenstand geben (wie oben) brauchen kein Komma!

In the office

1 ***Describe these people with a relative clause. You can use who or that.***

1 Steve / colleague / order our pens
Steve is the colleague who orders our pens.

2 Lucy / girl / sort / our mail

____

3 Mr Taylor / man / organize our meetings

____

4 Meg and Ryan / people / clean the office

____

5 My boss / woman / drive the blue car

____

2 ***Make one sentence out of two. Use who, which or that.***

1 I bought a new computer. It wasn't expensive.
We bought a new computer which wasn't expensive.

2 Phil brought in some cake. Everybody liked it.

____

3 Becky wrote an email. It was in German.

____

4 I talked to some customers. They were French.

____

3 ***Tick [✔] the sentences that <u>don't</u> need who or that.***

1 Ms Weber is the woman who I met at my interview. [ ]
2 Jackie is a girl who hates talking on the phone. [ ]
3 I had an accident with the car that I borrowed. [ ]
4 The office that they looked at was very small. [ ]
5 The colleagues who we met were French. [ ]

4 ***Only put in who, which or that where necessary.***

1 My colleague is a woman __________ hates computers.
2 The firm __________ I'm working for produces machines.
3 I need to write to the firm __________ opened on Graham Road.
4 The advert __________ we organized was a success.
5 My boss is one of those people __________ can't stand emails.

19 Quantifiers A

some/any – every/each, all (the)

A some/any

1 I'd like **some** apples, please. *(= einige / ein paar)*
I need **some** time. *(= etwas)*
- *some* bedeutet vor zählbaren Nomen „einige, ein paar", vor nicht zählbaren Nomen „etwas". (Im Deutschen kann auf das „etwas" verzichtet werden: „Ich brauche (etwas) Zeit.")

2 There aren't **any** birds in the garden.
I couldn't find **any** cheese in the fridge.
- In verneinten Aussagesätzen verwendet man *any* statt *some*. *not ... any* bedeutet dann „kein/keine".

3 Are there **any** questions?
Do you have **any** money?
Can I ask you **some** questions, please?
Would you like **some** bread?
- Man verwendet *any* auch oft in Fragen. Im Deutschen bleibt dies dann meist unübersetzt: „Gibt es (irgendwelche) Fragen?", „Hast du Geld?". In Bitten und Angeboten, die als Fragen formuliert sind, verwendet man jedoch *some*.

4 There's **somebody** in the house.
I can't see her **anywhere**.
- Was für *some* und *any* gilt, lässt sich auf die entsprechenden Zusammensetzungen (*somebody/anybody* bzw. *someone/anyone*, *something/anything* und *somewhere/anywhere*) übertragen.

B every/each, all (the)

1 We go to Spain **every** summer.
They give money to **each** school in the country.
- Sowohl *every* als auch *each* bedeuten „jede/r"; mit *each* hebt man hervor, dass jede einzelne bezeichnete Person oder Sache gemeint ist.

2 **All** pets have names.
I usually spend **all the** money that I earn.
- *all* bedeutet „alle/alles"; *all the* wird benutzt, wenn eine bestimmte Anzahl/Menge gemeint ist.

3 I'm tired. I've worked hard **all** day. *(= den ganzen Tag)*
Who's going to the party? – **All of us/them**! *(= wir/sie alle)*
The bus goes **every** 10 minutes. *(= alle 10 Minuten)*
- Beachte diese häufig gebrauchten Ausdrücke.

I'm a model!

1 ***Underline the quantifiers in the text and translate them into German below.***

Hello, my name is Sheena. I'm a model. Some people don't want to believe this, but it's true. I'm not very tall, my body looks quite normal. I don't worry about every piece of chocolate that I eat. But all the photographers who work with me want me back. And I love it – each time it's different, and each time it's fun. I don't have any money problems either. What's my secret [*Geheimnis*]?

1 ______________________
2 ______________________
3 ______________________
4 ______________________
5 ______________________

2 ***Sheena's secret. Translate the underlined phrases into German.***

Not every model [1] is a fashion model. Some models [2] never have to worry about their figure because nobody will see it. Instead they are careful the day before a photo shoot so that they don't get any problems [3] with their hands. Why? Because they're hand models! Sheena has perfect hands. When she started her career, her hands were photographed for hand cream adverts. Some photographers [4] quickly noticed how good she was at holding objects in front of the camera, so she became a film model too. You know all the TV adverts [5] where you see hands that are opening a can of food or washing up? Well, you could be looking at Sheena's hands...

1 ______________________
2 ______________________
3 ______________________
4 ______________________
5 ______________________

3a Complete the sentences with some or any.

1 We don't have ____________ fashion models.
2 Yes, there are also ____________ male hand models.
3 Sheena? She hasn't got ____________ time next week.
4 I even know ____________ actors who use hand models!
5 I'm sorry, I couldn't find ____________ hand models who are free tomorrow.
6 I could send you ____________ more photos.

3b Now circle some or any to complete these questions.

1 Could I ask you *some / any* questions, please?
2 Do you supply *some / any* foot models?
3 Would you like to see *some / any* photos?
4 May I suggest *some / any* other models?
5 Are there *some / any* problems with Sheena?
6 Are there *some / any* specific models that you're interested in?

4 Complete the sentences with one of the words from the box below.

some- any-	+	-body -thing -where

1 Sheena, ______________ phoned and wanted to book you.
2 I can't find my hand cream ________________ !
3 The studio is ________________ in the north.
4 I might have ________________ interesting for you.
5 I don't know ________________ at that studio.
6 He didn't know ________________ about modelling.

5 Tick whether each is right or wrong in the sentence.

		Right	Wrong
1	There are special models for each part of the body.	[ ]	[ ]
2	Each three months Sheena travels to New York.	[ ]	[ ]
3	Sheena has worked with each body part agency in Britain.	[ ]	[ ]
4	Each of the ten hand models here earns quite a lot of money.	[ ]	[ ]
5	Each candidate wants to win the modelling contract.	[ ]	[ ]

6 Complete the text with all, all the or all of us.

I sometimes work as a sports model so I have to look fit and healthy ________________ [1] time. It's fun, but it can also be stressful. Last summer I did a skiing photo shoot and we ________________ [2] had to start work at five in the morning because that's when the light is best. We couldn't choose what to wear from ________________ [3] nice clothes – we had to wear what they gave us. There was a lot of artificial [*künstlich*] snow and ________________ [4] had to stand on skis, with sticks in our hands. Then we had to pretend [*vorgeben*] that we were skiing. I don't even know how to ski! It was really stressful, and we had to wear different ski clothes ________________ [5] morning. We had fun in the breaks though when ________________ [6] models played in the snow.

7 Translate the following sentences.

1 Alle Mädchen wollen Supermodels werden.

____

2 Einige Jungen würden auch gern als Model arbeiten.

____

3 Aber nicht jedes Model kann ein Supermodel sein.

____

4 Die ganzen Modemodels sind viel zu dünn!

____

5 Modelagenturen suchen nach allen Arten [*kinds*] von Models.

____

6 Sie wollen Models für jeden Teil des Körpers.

____

7 Ohren, Augen, Füße, Hände – es gibt Models für alle Körperteile.

____

8 Möchtest du dir ein paar Agenturwebseiten anschauen?

____

20 Quantifiers B

a lot of (lots of) – many/much – few/little

A a lot of (lots of), many/much

1 **A lot of** people are worried about the environment.
There was **lots of** snow on the road.
- *a lot of* oder *lots of* bedeutet „(sehr) viele" (z. B. Menschen) oder „(sehr) viel" (z. B. Schnee).

2 I didn't send **many** emails yesterday.
I didn't have **much** time.
- *many* bedeutet „viele" und steht vor zählbaren *(countable)* Nomen. *much* bedeutet „viel" und steht vor nicht zählbaren *(non-countable)* Nomen.

3 Working for my old boss wasn't **much** fun.
There are **too many** problems with this project.
How much money do we need?
- Man verwendet *much/many* oft:
  – in verneinten Aussagesätzen
  – mit *as, so* oder *too* (= „so viel/e", „zu viel/e")
  – in Fragen *(How many/much?)*

4 We have **more** customers than the other firm.
Most employees here like their work.
- Will man „viel/e" steigern, verwendet man *more* und *most*.

B few/little

1 It only costs **a few** pounds.
It will only take **a little** time.
- *a few* bedeutet „einige, ein paar" und steht vor zählbaren Nomen. *a little* bedeutet „etwas, ein wenig" und steht vor nicht zählbaren Nomen.

2 few – fewer – fewest
little – less – least
- Beachte die Steigerungsformen.

3 There are very **few** men in this firm.
I earned very **little** money in my last job.
- *few* bedeutet „(nur) wenige" und steht vor zählbaren Nomen. *little* bedeutet „(nur) wenig" und steht vor nicht zählbaren Nomen. Beide Wörter werden häufig mit *very* verwendet.

Watch out!

„die meisten …" = *most*, niemals ~~*the*~~ *most*!

Comic Relief

Every two years, a lot of people around Britain take part in Red Nose Day. There are lots of events where people try to raise money [*Geld sammeln*] for Comic Relief, the organisation behind Red Nose Day. Most pupils pay a little money so that they don't have to wear school uniform on this day, for example. In the evening there's a big show on television with a lot of famous people. This is when Comic Relief raises most of the money. People know that they don't have to give much money. A lot of people just buy a red clown's nose, for example, and few people give nothing at all.

1 ***Read the text above and find the English translations of the phrases below.***

viele Menschen: ______________________

wenige Menschen: ______________________

viel Geld: ______________________

wenig Geld: ______________________

2 ***Complete the sentences with much or many.***

1 There are so ____________ ways to raise money.
2 You don't have to spend ____________ time.
3 Just organize as ____________ help as possible.
4 You can find so ____________ ideas on the Comic Relief website.
5 Remember: It doesn't have to be ____________ money.
6 Even a few pounds can help so ____________ poor people.

3 ***Cross out the wrong word or phrase to complete the sentences.***

1 There are so *a lot of / many* people who need our help.
2 No British charity organization raises as *a lot of / much* money as Comic Relief.
3 Too *a lot of / many* charities just ask for money.
4 There aren't *many / much* stars who say "no" to Comic Relief.
5 *A lot of / Much* schools raise money for Comic Relief on Red Nose Day.
6 How *a lot of / many* ways of raising money can you think of?

4 ***Red Nose Day is the best! Add more or most to write the sentences.***

1 Comic Relief / raises / money / than other charities
____
2 Red Nose Day / is / famous / than other charity events
____
3 people / wear / red noses / on Red Nose Day
____
4 Comic Relief / sells / red noses / than Red Nose Day T-shirts
____
5 children / have fun / on Red Nose Day
____

5 ***Who gets the money? Complete the sentences with little or few.***

1 Comic Relief helps people who have ________ money.
2 Comic Relief also supports projects in Britain, but ________ people realize that.
3 They help teenagers who have ________ hope of getting away from gangs, for example.
4 They also help African children who have ________ opportunities [*Chancen*] for an education, especially girls.
5 In some areas of Africa ________ girls even go to school.
6 Comic Relief trains teachers who have ________ knowledge about education for girls.

6 ***Complete the sentences with few, little or their comparative or superlative forms.***

1 There were ________ pupils at our Red Nose Day school event than we had hoped.
2 We had ________ time for the preparations than last year.
3 We had a maths quiz. The winner was the person who made the ________ mistakes.
4 The quiz made the ________ money of all the events in our school.
5 ________ pupils took part in it.
6 I'm afraid they had ________ fun.

7 ***(a) few or (a) little? Cross out the "a" where it's wrong. Then say what the underlined phrase means in German.***

1 I had <u>a few problems</u> with my red nose – it kept falling off my nose.
(German ________________)
2 This year I need <u>a little help</u> to organize the event. It's too much for one person.
(German ________________)
3 My colleagues had <u>very a few ideas</u> about what we could do to raise money. I need more than that!
(German ________________)
4 <u>A few ideas</u> weren't bad but they would have been too expensive.
(German ________________)
5 Now there's <u>a little time</u> left. We have to hurry.
(German ________________)
6 I think we need <u>a few more people</u> to help us. The more, the better!
(German ________________)

21 Prepositions

A Place and direction

1 The car is **in front of** the house.
Luca was standing **next to** Phil.

- Viele Präpositionen geben einen Ort an. Weitere Beispiele: *above, among, at, behind, between, in, inside, near, on, opposite, outside, round, under.*

2 I ran **up** the hill.
Latif climbed **onto** the horse.

- Mit Präpositionen lassen sich auch Richtungen benennen. Weitere Beispiele: *across, after, against, along, down, from, into, off, over, out of, past, through, to, towards.*

3 I was **at home** all afternoon. *(= zu Hause)*
I met him **at the party** last week. *(= auf der Party)*

- In manchen Fällen gibt es spezielle englische Wendungen mit Präpositionen, die man sich merken muss. Weitere Beispiele: *at school, at work, in the photo, in the world, on the beach, on the first floor, on the internet, on TV.*

B Time

1 Let's meet **at** 4 o'clock.
My sister was born **in** 2005.
I saw her **on** Saturday.

- In Zeitausdrücken werden oft die Präpositionen *at, in* oder *on* verwendet. Weitere Beispiele: *after, before, by, during, for, from … to, since, until/till, within.*

2 Three months **ago** I was in France.

- Mit *ago* sagt man, vor wie langer Zeit etwas geschah. *ago* steht immer hinter der Zeitangabe.

C Others

I saw a film **about** South Africa yesterday.
He couldn't play basketball **because of** his broken arm.

- Es gibt auch viele Präpositionen, die nicht im Zusammenhang mit Raum oder Zeit gebraucht werden. Weitere Beispiele: *against, for, instead of, like, per, with, without.*

Watch out!

near
near York (= bei York)
near the window (= nahe beim Fenster)
near the church (= in der Nähe der Kirche)

Paparazzi

1 ***I want to be a paparazzo. Find the prepositions (place/direction) and put them in the crossword.***

→

1 I live (*in der Nähe von*) Piccadilly Circus in London.
3 My flat is (*über*) a famous restaurant.
6 I often park my motorbike (*zwischen*) two trees.
7 I like driving (*durch*) London, although it's difficult to drive fast in the traffic.
10 I spend a lot of time (*in*) clubs, looking for famous people.
11 My friend often comes with me. He usually waits for me (*außerhalb*) the house.
12 On our way to the club we go (*… vorbei*) a cool bar, but I haven't seen any famous people there yet.

↓

2 Yesterday I ran (*hinter … her*) a woman who looked like a famous star – but it wasn't her.
4 My sports car is parked (*hinter*) the house.
5 My racing bike is usually leaning (*gegen*) the wall.
8 My cameras are always (*auf*) a special table near the door of my flat.
9 There's a famous club (*an*) the end of my street.

2 ***Paparazzi photos. Which is the right preposition (place/direction)? Cross out the wrong one.***

Paparazzi secretly take photos of famous people when they're…

1 … walking *through/towards* a city.
2 … eating *at/into* a restaurant.
3 … going *after/to* a gym.
4 … hiding *behind/between* sunglasses.
5 … coming *out of / outside* shops.

3 ***Which are the best hiding places for paparazzi? Look at the picture and complete the prepositions of place.***

1 ________ a table

2 ________ a roof

3 ________ two tourists

4 ________ a window

5 ________ a car

6 ________ a door

4 ***Find six prepositions of time in the text and write them next to their German translation.***

Mel Bouzad has been taking pictures of stars since he was seventeen. He moved from Britain to Los Angeles a few years ago with a camera bag and one suitcase. Now he has his own company there. He says the stars need the paparazzi too because they want to see their photos in the papers. His biggest sale was a photo of two stars during their breakup. Today he's chasing a famous singer. He jumps into his sports car to follow her, talking on his mobile. Seven photographers work for him. Their aim is to be there before the other photographers arrive. Now they're chasing the star's car. But they don't get the great pictures they wanted. They follow her till it gets dark, then they give up. After the chase, Mel tries to sell the pictures they took and is successful – even though they're boring pictures.

1 bevor: ________

2 bis: ________

3 nach: ________

4 seit: ________

5 vor: ________

6 während: ________

5 ***Tips for paparazzi. Tick [✔] the right preposition of time.***

		at	on	in	
1	She'll walk out of the house				3 p.m.
2	He'll be in Spain				September.
3	Can you be here				the evening?
4	Go to Milton's Hotel				Sunday morning.
5	She'll be on the plane to London				7 o'clock.
6	Be in my shop				April 3rd.

6 ***Complete the sentences with prepositions from the box.***

about • for • from • like • with • without

1 Stars understand that they have to live ________ the paparazzi.

2 They can never go anywhere ________ them.

3 But this is often quite OK ________ them – as long as they look good!

4 So the paparazzi may not be the only ones who profit ________ these photos.

5 It's different, of course, when the magazines write ________ bad things.

6 Then they want bad photos too, ________ a photo of a star crying.

7 ***Complete the English sentences using for, since or ago.***

1 *Paparazzo Mel wohnt seit 2006 in Los Angeles.*
Paparazzo Mel has lived in Los Angeles
________.

2 *Kim hat Mel vor einigen Tagen einen Tipp gegeben.*
Kim gave Mel a tip
________.

3 *Mel sucht diesen Star seit August.*
Mel has been looking for this star
________.

4 *Die Paparazzi folgen dem Star seit 2 Uhr.*
The paparazzi have been following the star
________.

5 *Ray fotografiert seit fünf Jahren Stars.*
Ray has been taking photos of stars
________.

6 *Er hatte vor zwei Monaten einen Unfall.*
He had an accident
________.

22 Conditional sentences

Mit Bedingungssätzen *(if-clauses)* kann man sagen, unter welchen Bedingungen etwas
– stattfindet *(type I)*,
– stattfinden würde *(type II)*,
– stattgefunden hätte *(type III)*.

If I **get** the new job, I**'ll earn** more money.
I**'ll earn** more money if I **get** the new job.

- Alle Bedingungssätze bestehen aus 2 Teilen: dem *if*-Nebensatz, der die Bedingung nennt, und dem Hauptsatz *(main clause)*, der feststellt, was sich aus der Bedingung ergibt. Steht der *if*-Teil des Satzes am Satzanfang, wird er durch ein Komma abgetrennt.

Type I

If it **rains**, we **won't go** by bike.
If you**'re** hungry, we **can get** some chips.

- Typ I der Bedingungssätze nennt eine erfüllbare Bedingung (= es ist durchaus möglich, dass die Bedingung erfüllt wird). Dabei steht der *if*-Satz im *simple present*; der Hauptsatz wird mit *will/won't* (oder einem anderen modalen Hilfsverb) + *infinitive* gebildet.

Type II

1 If I **had** enough money, I **would buy** that motorbike.

- Typ II der Bedingungssätze nennt eine kaum erfüllbare Bedingung (= es ist eher unwahrscheinlich oder sogar unmöglich, dass die Bedingung erfüllt wird). Dabei steht der *if*-Satz im *simple past*; der Hauptsatz wird mit *would/wouldn't* + *infinitive* gebildet.
- Im *if*-Teil steht das Verb im *simple past* – es wird aber nicht über die Vergangenheit gesprochen, sondern über eine Bedingung in der Gegenwart oder Zukunft.

2 If I **were** rich, I would buy a fast car.

- In Typ 2 Sätzen ist die Form des Verbs *be* für alle Personen immer *were*.

Type III

If you **had phoned** her, she **would have helped** you.

- Typ III nennt eine nicht mehr erfüllbare Bedingung (= die Chance, die Bedingung zu erfüllen, ist vorüber). Dabei steht der *if*-Satz im *past perfect*; der Hauptsatz wird mit *would/wouldn't have* + *past participle* gebildet.

Watch out!

Im *if*-Nebensatz steht nie *will* oder *would*!

The world of work

1 ***(Type I) Starting a job. Complete the main clauses using the notes in the box and will or won't.***

buy her a car • help me find a job • invite them to my party • not look for another job • not stay at the firm • wear his best clothes

1 If I like the work, I ______________________________ .
2 If my colleagues are nice, I ______________________________ .
3 If Jack doesn't like the job, he ______________________________ .
4 If she needs it for her job, Pam's father ______________________________ .
5 If Dan is invited to an interview, he ______________________________ .
6 If I ask my aunt, she ______________________________ .

2 ***(Type I) One word too many! Find the wrong word in each sentence and cross it out.***

1 I will have to travel a lot if I would get the job as a saleswoman.
2 If I will earn enough money, I can buy a better car.
3 I will need lots of clothes if I will have to stay in hotels all the time.
4 If I would spend more money on clothes, I won't have enough for food.
5 I won't have time for sports if I will have to travel all the time.
6 If I would get up early enough, I can go jogging.
7 If I will get a new job, I will go on holiday to Barbados next year.
8 I will learn lots of new things if I will go to this seminar.

3 ***(Type II) Tick the right answer.***

1 If I were my own boss, …
a [ ] The person is his own boss.
b [ ] The person isn't his own boss.

2 If I worked in an office, …
a [ ] The person works in an office.
b [ ] The person doesn't work in an office.

3 If the computer worked, …
a [ ] The computer works.
b [ ] The computer doesn't work.

4 ***(Type II) Complete the sentences with the right form of the verb in brackets.***

1 Tina would already be rich if she ______________ (work) as a model.

2 If she ______________ (find) a job in Los Angeles, she would move to the USA.

3 If her boyfriend Tom ______________ (come) with her, they'd have a great time.

4 If Tom ______________ (be) a pilot, he'd be able to see the whole world.

5 His parents would be very happy if he ______________ (have) such a good job.

6 He wouldn't be sad if Tina ______________ (go) to LA because he could go and see her often.

5 ***(Type I/II) Help! The computer is broken. Circle the right word.***
Tip: Look at the main clause.

1 If the computer *isn't / wasn't* repaired by tomorrow, I won't be able to finish my project in time.

2 I know the computer is old. I wouldn't work with it if I *didn't have to / don't have to*.

3 If Lucy *is / were* here, she'd know what to do.

4 I'd help you if I *knew / know* how.

5 I'll send Lucy an email if you *think / thought* that's OK.

6 I'd repair the computer if I *had / have* the time.

7 If the boss *comes / came*, we won't tell her anything.

8 If we *are / were* lucky, we'll fix it ourselves.

6 ***(Type I/II) Complete the sentences with the right form of the verbs in English.***

1 If she's busy now, I ______________ (*anrufen*) her again later.

2 What would you do if you ______________ (*sein*) the boss here?

3 If it's OK with you, I ______________ (*benutzen*) your computer when you're on holiday.

4 I ______________ (*sprechen*) to the boss if someone were bullying me.

5 If I don't go now, I ______________ (*verpassen*) the bus.

7 ***(Type III) Complete the sentences. Use the words above the sentences.***

1 ~~applied~~ • got • ~~had~~ • have • would

If Tom *had applied* for the job earlier, he ______________ it.

2 had • had • have • worked • wouldn't

If Lisa ______________ harder at school, she ______________ so many problems later.

3 chosen • had • have • known • would

If I ______________ how stressful this job is, I ______________ a different career.

4 had • have • repaired • saved • would

If we ______________ the machine ourselves, we ______________ a lot of money.

5 done • had • have • told • wouldn't

If my boss ______________ me what to do, I ______________ the wrong thing.

8 ***(Type I/II/III) Finish the sentences with the right form of the verb in the main clause.***

1 If my teacher hadn't told me about the job, I ______________ (not know) about it.

2 If I were better at maths, I ______________ (be) an electrician.

3 If I look on the internet, I ______________ (find) a job.

4 If you had seen the old building, you ______________ (not go) in either.

5 If my brother had more time, he ______________ (help) me with my application.

6 If I find a job quickly, I ______________ (be able to) afford that new skirt.

23 Reported speech

1 "**I called**." ▸ Pam told me (that) **she had called**.

Mit der indirekten Rede gibt man wieder, was jemand anders gesagt hat. Sie wird durch Verben wie *say, tell, answer*, usw. und dem Wort *that* eingeleitet; *that* kann meist auch entfallen. Außerdem muss der Wortlaut angepasst werden; das betrifft vor allem Pronomen sowie die Zeitform des Verbs.

2 "What are you doing?" ▸ He **asked what** I was doing.
"Did Ben like the music?"
▸ She **asked if/whether** Ben had liked the music.

Fragen werden in der indirekten Rede mit *ask* oder einem ähnlichen Verb und einem Fragepronomen (*what, why, who,* usw.) oder dem Wort *if* bzw. *whether* eingeleitet.

3 "I'm hungry." ▸ Ben **says** (that) he's hungry.

Steht das einleitende Verb im *simple present* gibt es keine Zeitverschiebung.

4 simple present ▸ simple past:
"It's cold." ▸ He said **it was** cold.
present progressive ▸ past progressive:
"**I'm doing** my homework." ▸ She said she **was doing** her homework."
simple past ▸ past perfect:
"I **met** her in town." ▸ She said she **had met** her in town.
present perfect ▸ past perfect:
"I**'ve** just **seen** him." ▸ He said he **had** just **seen** him.
will ▸ would:
"Joe **will** help us." ▸ She said Joe **would** help us.

Wenn man die indirekte Rede durch ein Verb im *simple past* ein leitet, muss das, was gesagt wurde, zeitlich noch weiter zurückversetzt werden.

5 "Paul is leaving **this** afternoon," she said.
▸ She said Paul was leaving **that** afternoon.

Auch Zeitadverbien müssen bei dieser Form der indirekten Rede angepasst werden, damit ihr Sinn erhalten bleibt. Weitere Beispiele: *now* ▸ *right away*; ~~*today*~~ then ▸ *that day*; *tomorrow* ▸ *the next day*; *yesterday* ▸ *the day before*, *two days ago* ▸ *two days before*; *next year* ▸ *the following year*.

Watch out!

Nach *tell* nennt man die Person, der etwas gesagt wurde. Wird die Person nicht genannt, verwendet man *say* z.B. *He **told** me that* …
ABER *He **said** that* …

Fun at the camp

1 ***Who says what? Complete the sentences with information from the photo above.***

1 The girl on the left says that that is the best time of her life.
2 The boy on the right says that he has met so many amazing people there.
3 The girl in the middle says that she really hopes she'll be able to go again next year.
4 The boy in the middle says that he can play the guitar then.

2 ***Read the dialogue and then complete the sentences about the questions that Sharon's mum has.***

Sharon	Mum, can I spend my summer holidays at the youth camp, please?
Mum	Well, I don't know. Where is it?
Sharon	It's on the coast.
Mum	And how many teenagers will be there?
Sharon	I really don't know. Maybe two or three hundred.
Mum	Do the teenagers come from all over the world?
Sharon	Yes, it's an international camp.
Mum	What age will they be?
Sharon	You have to be between 16 and 21.
Mum	Do they offer lots of activities at the camp?
Sharon	Oh yes, they do. They offer lots of outdoor activities and workshops.
Mum	And now the most important question: How much does it cost?
Sharon	I don't know, but I'll ask Laura. She was there last year.

1 Sharon asked her mother if she could spend her summer holidays at the youth camp.
2 Her mother wanted to know where it was .
3 She also asked how many teenagers would be there.
4 She asked if the teenagers came from all over the world.
5 And she asked what age they would be .
6 Then she wanted to know if they offer lot of at the camp.
7 And finally she asked how much it cost .

3 *Camp activities. Correct the time phrases.*

1 Matt said that he had done some climbing ~~yesterday~~.
the day before.
2 Gracie told me that she was playing the guitar ~~today~~.
that day.
3 David asked who was going bowling ~~tomorrow~~.
the following day
4 Becky wanted to know who was taking part in the workshop ~~this evening~~.
that evening

4 *Sharon's email. Read Sharon's email and put in say or tell in the right tense.*

Tip: Look at the second part of the sentences.

New email
Send Chat Attach Addresses Fonts Save

Dear Laura,

I'm writing because you've been to a youth camp before. You told [1] me afterwards that it had been fantastic. And now I would like to go to a summer camp. Didn't you tell [2] me that the camp was called 'CoolCamps on the Coast'? I've looked at their website and it looks good. It says [3] there that they're still looking for people to join them this summer. And you said [4] that it wasn't too expensive, didn't you? I've also looked at their guest book. A lot of interesting people from all over the world left messages there. Most of them said [5] that they had had so much fun together at the last camp. My parents told [6] me I would be allowed to go if it wasn't too expensive. Please write back as soon as possible. Thanks! I'm so excited :-))

Lots of love, Sharon

5 *Complete the sentences with the right form of the verbs in brackets.*

1 Mum, Laura answered my email. She wrote that she had been (be) at the camp two years ~~ago~~ before.
2 She told me that she had met (meet) so many interesting people from around the world.
3 She also said that they were (be) still in email contact.
4 Laura even said that she would probably go (probably go) to Spain next summer to visit one of them.
5 She told me she had started (start) to learn judo there.
6 Finally she said she couldn't (can not) remember the price, but she knew it hadn't been too much.

6 *Put these comments from people who have been to the camp into reported speech.*

1 *"Camp is the best way to spend the summer." (Charlie)*
Charlie wrote that the camp was the best .
2 *"I really hope I can come again." (Rose)*
She really hoped she could come again.
3 *"I'm listening to the camp song!" (Mike)*
Mike
4 *"I had such a great time!" (Silvia)*
She had had a great time.
5 *"I didn't get the camp DVD." (Sagiv)*
He haven't give the camp DVD.
6 *"I've just received the DVD." (Eddie)*
He had just recived the DVD.
7 *"I've just had an email from Tommy." (Debby)*
She had just had an email from Tommy.
8 *"We'll be able to see the DVD on the camp website." (Tina)*
Tina said that we would be able to see the DVD on the camp web-site.

24 Passive

A General

1 Thousands of cars **are sold** every day.
- Mit einem Passivsatz sagt man, dass etwas mit einem Gegenstand oder einer Person gemacht wird/wurde. Die Passivform wird mit einer Form von *be* und dem *past participle* des Verbs gebildet.

2 The cups **are made** of plastic.
A car **was stolen** yesterday.
The church **was built** in 1608.
- Mit dem Passiv kann man über Handlungen sprechen, ohne deren Urheber bzw. Ursache zu nennen, z.B. wenn es nicht wichtig ist oder wenn man nicht weiß, wer die Handlung ausführte, oder wenn die Handlung (und nicht die handelnde Person) im Mittelpunkt steht.

3 (Aktivsatz) Amy McDonald wrote this song.
(Passivsatz) This song was written **by** Amy McDonald.
- Mit *by* kann man Informationen über Urheber bzw. Ursache der Handlung hinzufügen.

4 Breakfast **can** be ordered until 11 a.m.
- Oft wird das Passiv auch mit Hilfsverben gebildet: Hilfsverb + Form von *be* + *past participle*.

5 The seats are **not** made in this firm.
This oil is**n't** used for cooking.
- Die Verneinung erfolgt mit *not*.

B Tenses

- Das Passiv kann mit allen Zeitformen gebildet werden:
(1) simple present: Football **is played** in lots of countries.
(2) simple past: Our car **was repaired** last week.
(3) present perfect: These houses **have** just **been built**.
(4) past perfect: The houses **had** just **been built** when I moved here.
(5) future: Your room **will be cleaned** as soon as possible.

Watch out!

Wo im Englischen das Passiv benutzt wird, steht im Deutschen oft „man": „*I was asked to bring a salad.*" (= Man bat mich, einen Salat mitzubringen.)

Joel's restaurant

Joel's story

"I was born in 1990. I was sent to a special school when I was 7. Everybody said I was stupid, so I believed them. There was a boy gang in my neighbourhood. One day I was asked by the boss of the gang if I wanted to be a member. I said yes. But first I had to do a dare [*Mutprobe*]. I was given a gun and I was told to shoot a little dog that belonged to an old man in the street. I'm sorry to say that I did it. A day later the old man was found in his flat, dead. He had killed himself. I felt really bad but I didn't have the courage to leave the gang. When I was 16, I was chosen to be one of the gang's drug dealers. Everything was crazy with drugs and fighting. We were caught by the police in the end though."

1 ***Find the passive phrases in the text above and translate them into German.***

1 *I was born* — *ich wurde geboren*
2 ________ ________
3 ________ ________
4 ________ ________
5 ________ ________
6 ________ ________
7 ________ ________
8 ________ ________

2 ***Complete the sentences about Joel's time in prison [Gefängnis] with the simple past passive.***

1 Joel ________ (visit) regularly by a social worker.
2 Joel ________ (tell) about school lessons and practical training [*Ausbildung*].

3 Joel had always liked cooking. Here he ________ (teach) how to cook for big groups of people.

4 Other activities, like a computer club, ________ (also offer) in prison.

5 Because Joel did well, he ________ (give) the chance to surf the internet to get ideas for his future.

6 In the end Joel ________ (introduce) to an organization which helps people like him.

3 ***The restaurant. Cross out the wrong form.***

1 Joel *was given / has been* given a business loan [*Geschäftskredit*] when he left prison.

2 The loan *was spent / has been* spent on renting a restaurant and buying some equipment and food.

3 The restaurant *was owned / had been owned* by an Italian, so there were lots of things to do to change it into a Caribbean restaurant.

4 After the walls *were painted / had been* painted in bright colours, reggae CDs *were bought / had been* bought.

5 Just before the opening, kitchen staff *were hired / have been hired* and trained.

4 ***Active or passive? Tick the correct sentences about Joel's staff.***

1 [ ] **a** The young men and women recommended to Joel by the prison.
[ ] **b** The young men and women were recommended to Joel by the prison.

2 [ ] **a** About 20 prisoners [*Gefangene*] interviewed.
[ ] **b** About 20 prisoners were interviewed.

3 [ ] **a** Joel hired six of them.
[ ] **b** Joel was hired six of them.

4 [ ] **a** When they leave prison, they will lose their jobs.
[ ] **b** When they leave prison, they will be lost their jobs.

5 [ ] **a** But they will hire by other restaurants because of their experience.
[ ] **b** But they will be hired by other restaurants because of their experience.

6 [ ] **a** Their jobs will then give to other prisoners.
[ ] **b** Their jobs will then be given to other prisoners.

5 ***Write passive sentences. Be careful with the tenses.***

1 the meals in the restaurant / prepare / by prisoners

____

2 the restaurant / can book / for birthday parties

____

3 Joel's restaurant / mention / in an article last week

____

4 the restaurant / give / a good review in the article

____

5 Joel's restaurant / just vote / 'Best restaurant of the year'

____

6 a second restaurant / open / next year

____

6 ***Read the signs and then complete the passive sentences. You will need the verbs in the box.***

can order • ~~can send~~ • close • require • serve

Vacancy: ***Bar staff needed***

1 Applications *can be sent* to joel.restaurant@freeway.co.uk.

Opening times
Tues – Sun 11 a.m. – 2 a.m.

2 The restaurant ________ on Monday.

Takeway orders:
Tel. 367 893

3 Takeaways ________ on 367 893.

To buy alcohol,
you must have ID.

4 ID ________ to buy alcohol.

Last food orders: 12 p.m.

5 Food ________ until 12 p.m.

Test 4

Relative clauses (▸ S. 51)

1 ***Complete the sentences with the right relative pronoun.***

1 Mary cooked a healthy meal ______________ tasted great.
2 "Princess" is the little dog ______________ belongs to our neighbours.
3 Patty is the girl ______________ lives across the road.
4 I bought a car ______________ was very cheap.
5 My colleague is a man ______________ hurts himself a lot.

2 ***Cross out the word or words that are not needed.***
Careful: Some sentences need all their words!

1 I'm going to save the money that I earn for a new bike.
2 Lou designs T-shirts that sell quite well.
3 The trees that are growing in this garden are very old.
4 Karen is the colleague who I admire most.
5 Pete is the boy who I like best in my class.
6 Josh is driving the car that Mike sold him.
7 Mel is the colleague who helps everybody.
8 The woman who answered the phone seemed young.

Quantifiers A (▸ S. 52)

3 ***Circle the right word in each sentence or question.***

1 My sister met *any / some* nice people in Italy.
2 Pam spent her holidays *anywhere / somewhere* in Spain.
3 Our son doesn't have *any / some* friends here yet.
4 Excuse me, do you sell *any / some* used games?
5 I just don't have *any / some* time at the moment.
6 Shouldn't we buy *any / some* cake for later?
7 If you like, I could lend you *any / some* money.
8 I couldn't find *anybody / somebody* who knew the answer.

4 ***Correct any wrong sentences.***

1 Can you give me any help please?
____

2 I don't have some money.
____

3 Would you like some bread?
____

4 I've got hardly some time this week.
____

5 ***Finish the sentences with each (where possible) or every.***

1 I know ______________ dog in the neighbourhood.
2 There were cars parked on ______________ side of the street.
3 The boss spoke to ______________ of the employees.
4 There's a plane to Sydney ______________ third day.
5 I enjoyed ______________ minute of the film.
6 I was carrying a cup of tea in ______________ hand when the phone rang.

6 ***all or all the? Tick [✔] the right start of the sentence.***

	All	All the	
1			cars are bad for the environment.
2			new cars that I've heard of use less petrol.
3			houses need fresh paint from time to time.
4			houses in this street are old.
5			customers on this list have to be called.
6			customers will have to wait a bit.
7			firms have had a difficult year.
8			firms in our area are struggling.

Quantifiers B (▸ S. 54)

7 ***Finish the sentences with much, many, more or most.***

1 We didn't get ______________ letters today.
2 I know ______________ jokes than you!
3 Don't put too ______________ sugar in my tea, please.
4 There weren't ______________ people at the party last night.
5 How ______________ money do you need?
6 ______________ students in our class like ice cream (more than 80%).

8 ***Complete the sentences with the right English phrase.***

1 Very ______________ (*wenige*) colleagues in the firm go out for lunch.

2 We may have to get ______________ (*ein paar*) more chairs for the party.

3 If you have ______________ (*ein wenig*) time, come by for a cup of tea.

4 We had so ______________ (*wenig*) fun in our holidays – it rained all the time.

5 There are ______________ (*weniger*) bottles left than I thought.

6 I like very ______________ (*wenige*) of Jack's friends.

Prepositions (▸ S. 56)

9 ***Complete the sentences using the opposite preposition.***

1 I always park my bike in front of the house, but Sue parks her bike ______________ the house.

2 When I walk over the bridge, Sue walks ______________ it.

3 I always have lunch inside the house, but Sue eats ______________ when it isn't raining.

4 Every time I go into the kitchen, Sue comes ______________ it.

5 Every time I ride my bike up the hill, Sue rides ______________ it.

6 I usually cycle around the town centre, but Sue always cycles ______________ it.

10 ***Complete the sentences with the right preposition from the box.***

ago • during • for • from • since • within

1 I'll stay in Manchester ______________ two more months.

2 Mark works in London ______________ Monday to Saturday.

3 I met them ______________ my time in New York.

4 Lucy must find a new job ______________ three months.

5 I've worked here ______________ last summer.

6 The customer said she phoned two weeks ______________ .

11 ***Complete the phrases with the right prepositions.***

1 I had lunch ________ work today.

2 I think I have the best job ________ the world!

3 I ordered some books ________ the internet.

4 I saw an interesting programme ________ TV last night.

5 Can you see Fred ________ the photo?

6 Where's your daughter? – She's ________ school.

7 I spent my holiday ________ the beach in Italy.

8 My office is ________ the second floor.

Conditional sentences (▸ S. 58)

12 ***(Type II) Write sentences about these people's dreams.***
Remember: These things probably won't happen.

1 Lea: be a doctor / be very happy
If Lea were a doctor, she would be very happy.

2 Phil: live in California / be a rich man

____

3 Jane: have lots of money / give it to poor children

____

4 Luke: not play in a band / not be very happy

____

5 Matt: not be Lisa's boyfriend / Sarah go out with him

____

13 ***(Type I/II) Cross out the wrong verb forms.***
Tip: Read the conditions in German carefully!

1 What *will/would* you buy if someone *gives/gave* you £100?
(*Das macht aber sowieso keiner.*)

2 If *there is / there were* a good film on TV on Saturday night, *I'll/I'd* stay at home.
(*Samstags kommen oft gute Filme.*)

3 Dennis *will/would* wear his best suit if *he is / he were* invited for an interview.
(*Er hat aber schon viele Absagen erhalten.*)

4 If I *have/had* more time, *I'll/I'd* stay longer.
(*Aber der nächste Termin wartet schon.*)

5 If the best MP3 player *is/were* too expensive, *I'll/I'd* buy a cheaper one.
(*Ich habe nicht viel Geld.*)

14 *(Type I/II/III) Match the two parts of the sentences.*

1	If it snows,	a	I wouldn't spend it.
2	If he had phoned us,	b	I'd have believed her.
3	If I met Ben again,	c	we won't wait for you
4	If you had hurried,	d	you'd have got the bus.
5	If I found some money,	e	we'll go skiing.
6	If you're late,	f	we'd have picked him up.
7	If I see Anna,	g	I wouldn't talk to him.
8	If I hadn't known better,	h	I'll tell her about the job.

Reported speech (► S. 60)

15 *Change the pronouns and the adverbs of time to complete the sentences.*

1 "I'm repairing my car this afternoon."
Joe said that ________ was repairing ________ car ________________ afternoon.

2 "We worked till 7 p.m. yesterday."
My colleagues said that ________ had worked till 7 p.m. ________________ .

3 "I'll take the train to London tomorrow."
Ms Keanes said that ________ would take the train to London ________________ .

4 "Are you going on holiday next month?"
My boss asked me if ________ was going on holiday ________________ .

5 "I'm phoning my mum tonight."
Kylie said that ________ was phoning ________ mum ________________ .

16 *But you said … ! Change the verbs in brackets into the right verb form in reported speech.*

1 You said it ________________ (is) hot outside – it's not!
2 Layla said that she ________________ (has seen) a great dress in town.
3 I said that I ________________ (will) pick you up at 4, not 5!
4 Aysha told me she ________________ (is) washing her hair when I phoned.
5 Murat answered that he ________________ (talked) to Ken the day before.
6 Jerry told us that Becky ________________ (goes) out with Tim.

Passive (► S. 62)

17 *Complete the sentences with the English equivalent of the German in brackets.*

1 Breakfast ________________ (*wurde serviert*) in the room.
2 The room ________________ (*wurde sauber gemacht*) every day.
3 Fresh flowers ________________ (*wurden gestellt*) on the table every morning.
4 If we wanted to go anywhere, a car ________________ (*wurde geschickt*) to the hotel.

18 *Write passive sentences. Be careful of the tense.*

1 The thief / see / in town last week
____

2 Careful! / This fence / just paint
____

3 The room / just clean / when we arrived
____

4 My bike / repair / next week
____

19 *Complete the English sentences. Use the passive.*

1 *Man bat mich, einen Kuchen zu backen.*
________________________ to make a cake.

2 *Man fragte Tim, ob er dem Verein beitreten wollte.*
________________________ if he wanted to join the club.

3 *Man gab mir ein paar Blumen.*
________________________ some flowers.

4 *Man benutzt diese Creme* [cream] *nicht im Gesicht.*
________________________ on the face.

Unregelmäßige Verben

Grundform	Vergangenheit	3. Form	Bedeutung
be	was/were	been	sein
become	became	become	werden
begin	began	begun	anfangen
bring	brought	brought	bringen
build	built	built	bauen
buy	bought	bought	kaufen
catch	caught	caught	fangen
choose	chose	chosen	wählen
come	came	come	kommen
cost	cost	cost	kosten
do	did	done	tun, machen, erledigen
drink	drank	drunk	trinken
drive	drove	driven	fahren, (aus)treiben
eat	ate	eaten	essen, fressen
fall	fell	fallen	fallen
feel	felt	felt	(sich) fühlen
fight	fought	fought	kämpfen
find	found	found	finden
fly	flew	flown	fliegen
forget	forgot	forgotten	vergessen
go	went	gone	gehen
get	got	got	bekommen, erhalten
grow	grew	grown	wachsen
have	had	had	haben
hear	heard	heard	hören
hide	hid	hidden	verstecken
hit	hit	hit	schlagen, aufprallen auf
hold	held	held	halten
hurt	hurt	hurt	verletzen
keep	kept	kept	behalten
know	knew	known	kennen, wissen
lead	led	led	führen
leave	left	left	verlassen
let	let	let	lassen
lose	lost	lost	verlieren
make	made	made	machen
mean	meant	meant	bedeuten, sagen wollen
meet	met	met	sich treffen
pay	paid	paid	(be-)zahlen
put	put	put	setzen, stellen, legen
read	read	read	lesen
ring	rang	rung	läuten, klingeln, anrufen
rise	rose	risen	steigen
run	ran	run	laufen
say	said	said	sagen
see	saw	seen	sehen
sell	sold	sold	verkaufen
send	sent	sent	senden, schicken
sit	sat	sat	sitzen
sleep	slept	slept	schlafen
speak	spoke	spoken	sprechen
spend	spent	spent	ausgeben, verbringen (Zeit)
stand	stood	stood	stehen
take	took	taken	nehmen
teach	taught	taught	unterrichten, lehren
tell	told	told	erzählen, mitteilen, sagen
think	thought	thought	denken, meinen
understand	understood	understood	verstehen
wake	woke	woken	wecken
write	wrote	written	schreiben

Zeitentabelle

Die Zeitentabelle veranschaulicht das englische Zeitensystem. Sie enthält eine Beispielform eines englischen Verbs, die deutsche Übersetzung desselben und die verneinte sowie die Frageform. Die Zeitentabelle gibt jedoch nur einen groben Überblick über die englischen Verbformen und deren deutsche Entsprechungen. Detaillierter sind die Erläuterungen in den entsprechenden Units in *Spotlight on Grammar*.

Aktiv

Zeiten	Formen	Verneinungen	Fragen	deutsch
Present				
simple	I work	I don't work	Do you work?	*ich arbeite*
continuous	I am working	I'm not working	Are you working?	*ich arbeite gerade*
Past				
simple	I worked	I didn't work	Did you work?	*ich arbeitete*
continuous	I was working	I wasn't working	Were you working?	*ich arbeitete gerade*
Present perfect				
simple	I have worked	I haven't worked	Have you worked?	*ich habe gearbeitet*
continuous	I have been working	I haven't been working	Have you been working?	*ich habe gerade gearbeitet*
Past perfect				
simple	I had worked	I hadn't worked	Had you worked?	*ich hatte gearbeitet*
continuous	I had been working	I hadn't been working	Had you been working?	*ich hatte gerade gearbeitet*
Future				
simple	I will work	I won't work	Will you work?	*ich werde arbeiten*
continuous	I will be working	I won't be working	Will you be working?	*ich werde gerade arbeiten*
perfect	I will have worked	I won't have worked	Will you have worked?	*ich werde gearbeitet haben*
Conditional				
simple	I would work	I wouldn't work	Would you work?	*ich würde arbeiten*
perfect	I would have worked	I wouldn't have worked	Would you have worked?	*ich würde gearbeitet haben*

Passiv

Zeiten	Formen	Verneinungen	Fragen	deutsch
Present				
simple	I am asked	I'm not asked	Are you asked?	*ich werde gefragt*
continuous	I am being asked	I'm not being asked	Are you being asked?	*ich werde gerade gefragt*
Past				
simple	I was asked	I was asked	Were you asked?	*ich wurde gefragt*
continuous	I was being asked	I wasn't being asked	Were you being asked?	*ich wurde gerade gefragt*
Present perfect				
	I have been asked	I haven't been asked	Have you been asked?	*ich bin gefragt worden*
Past perfect				
	I had been asked	I hadn't been asked	Had you been asked?	*ich war gefragt worden*
Future				
	I will be asked	I won't be asked	Will you be asked?	*ich werde gefragt werden*
Conditional				
	I would be asked	I wouldn't be asked	Would you be asked?	*ich würde gefragt werden*

SPO
TLI
GHT

SPOTLIGHT ON GRAMMAR

Arbeitsbuch zur Wiederholung grammatischer Grundstrukturen

LÖSUNGEN

Cornelsen

Spotlight on Grammar – Seite **4**

1 Nouns and articles

1a

restaurants, meals, tips, cafés, noodles, restaurants, salads, vegetables, people, pizzas, children, restaurants, curries, dishes

1b

dishes – dish; curries – curry; people – person; children – child

2

1 Burgers, people, chips; **2** variety, day, parties; **3** meals, waiters, sandwiches; **4** fish, potatoes, dream

Spotlight on Grammar – Seite **5**

3

1 breakfasts; **2** eggs; **3** sausages; **4** tomatoes; **5** pieces; **6** glasses; **7** cups; **8** strawberries

4

1 month; **2** sheriff; **3** tomato; **4** foot; **5** child

5

1 are; **2** Are; **3** is; **4** is; **5** are; **6** is

6

Pam's, country's, tourists', London's, cousin's

7

1 children's; **2** parents'; **3** Peter's; **4** men's; **5** Jess'

8

1 a; **2** an; **3** an; **4** a; **5** an; **6** a; **7** a; **8** a; **9** a; **10** an; **11** a; **12** an

9

1 a, -, -; **2** a, a, a, -; **3** -, a, a; **4** an, -, -; **5** -, -, -, a, -; **6** -, -, a

Spotlight on Grammar – Seite **6**

2 Pronouns A

1

personal pronouns: I, it, I, It, we, we, we, I, she, she, she, I, I, I, I; possessive pronouns: My, My, mine; reflexive pronouns: ourselves, yourself

2

1 I, my; **2** me, I; **3** I, myself, my, mine; **4** myself, me, I

Spotlight on Grammar – Seite **7**

3

1 her; **2** us; **3** them; **4** it; **5** them; **6** him

4

1 my; **2** his; **3** her; **4** her; **5** me; **6** it

5

1 b; **2** d; **3** e; **4** a; **5** f; **6** c

6

1 they; **2** their; **3** Our; **4** us; **5** our; **6** we; **7** you; **8** yourself; **9** me; **10** We; **11** us; **12** You, **13** you; **14** our

7

1 They're, their; **2** It's, its; **3** you're, your; **4** theirs, there's

Spotlight on Grammar – Seite **8**

3 Pronouns B

1

1 these; **2** those; **3** This; **4** that; **5** one, one

2

1 … this one or that one?
2 Where can I find the best ones?
3 This is a black one and that's a blue one.
4 … two old skirts and a new one …
5 Which one? The one that Paul wrote or the one from school?

3

1 This is Ella's bike. And that's her coat.
2 These houses here are old. Those ones over there are new.

3 I like these dresses more than those ones.
4 These CDs cost £10 and those ones cost £15.

Spotlight on Grammar – Seite **9**

Spotlight on... Word order

1

1 Paula never has any money.
2 She always spends everything she gets.
3 But Danny sometimes saves his money.
4 He usually spends very little.
5 So Paula often tries to borrow money from Danny.
6 But Danny says no because he knows he'll never get it back.

2

1 Right
2 Wrong. We put our things on some tables around the youth club.
3 Wrong. It was a great success.
4 Right
5 Wrong. "It's great that we can buy cheap things here," they said.
6 Wrong. We gave part of the money to a church project.

Spotlight on Grammar – Seite **10**

4 The verb 'be'

1

There's, it's, They're, they're, There's, there's, there're, Here's, it's, They're

2

1 is, **2** is, **3** are; **4** are; **5** are; **6** is; **7** is; **8** is; **9** is; **10** are

Spotlight on Grammar – Seite **11**

3

1 c; **2** a, **3** b; **4** f; **5** e; **6** d

4

1 isn't, is; **2** are, are not, are; **3** is, isn't, is; **4** 're not, are, 'm not, 'm

5

2 they are; **3** I'm not; **4** I am; **5** it is; **6** they're not

6

1 was; **2** wasn't; **3** was; **4** was; **5** were; **6** weren't; **7** wasn't; **8** were; **9** was; **10** was

7

2 Were there lots of cool bands?
3 Were there thousands of fans?
4 Were the fans loud?
5 Was there anybody over 18 there?
6 Was the organizer happy?

8

1 were; **2** were; **3** were; **4** was; **5** was

Spotlight on Grammar – Seite **12**

5 The verb 'have'

1

2 They have got a flat ...
3 He has a digital camera ...
4 ... he doesn't have a pet.
5 ... they haven't got a garden.
6 ... he always has time to write.

2

1 Do you have / Have you got...
2 Do you have / Have you got ...
3 Does your friend have / Has your friend got ...
4 Do you have / Have you got ...
5 Do you have / Have you got ...
6 Does your flat have / Has your flat got ...

3

1 doesn't have; **2** don't have; **3** doesn't have; **4** don't have

Spotlight on Grammar – Seite **13**

4

1 Laura has 10 e-pals.
2 I don't have as many e-pals as Laura.
3 I have got 6 e-pals.
4 I only had 4 e-pals last year.
5 My e-pal Jason has a new dog.
6 He didn't have a dog when I started writing to him.

5

1 e; **2** d; **3** b; **4** f; **5** c; **6** a

6

1 Yes, she does; **2** Yes, he has; **3** Yes, she has; **4** No, they don't; **5** Yes, they have

7

1 My brother has an e-pal.
2 Do you have / Have you got an e-pal?
3 Richtig
4 … Yes, she did.
5 We had a house but we have now got a flat.

8

1 Did you have; **2** did you have; **3** Did you have; **4** Did you have; **5** did you have; **6** did they have

9

1 d; **2** c; **3** a; **4** e; **5** h, **6** b; **7** f; **8** g

Spotlight on Grammar – Seite **14**

6 Simple present

1

infinitive form: be, want, spend, live, drive, smile, earn;
third person s: wants, worries, criticizes, tries, gets;
negative form: don't worry, don't work, don't want, doesn't lead

2

2 Robbi sings.
3 Mustafa and Paolo play football.
4 Kim plays the guitar.
5 Mel takes photos.
6 Gordon and Julie cook.

Spotlight on Grammar – Seite **15**

3

Simon, the superstar
He wakes up late in the morning. He doesn't get up – he has breakfast in bed. He listens to some music and then he takes a walk around his garden. He swims in the pool for a while. Then he calls his driver and he gets into a big white car. He does some shopping in town and he gives lots of autographs. He doesn't worry about the money that he spends because he has enough. In the evening he meets some interesting rich people for dinner and he goes to bed really late.

4a

1 Do you always get up late?
2 Does your butler make your breakfast?
3 Do you have a big pool?
4 Does your driver do other jobs too?
5 Do you ever worry about money?

4b

1 No, I don't.
2 No, I don't.
3 Yes, I do.
4 Yes, he does.
5 No, I don't.

5

2 do I need; **3** has; **4** makes; **5** do you prepare; **6** do you earn

6

2 They always have to keep fit.
3 Most of them never drink alcohol.
4 An actor is often away from home for months.
5 A football star usually trains for five hours a day.
6 But they have a great holiday once a year.

7

1 eat; **2** tries; **3** writes; **4** misses; **5** stay; **6** leaves

Spotlight on Grammar – Seite **16**

7 Present progressive

1

I'm talking, She's just writing, We're watching, He's chatting, They're just surfing, I'm not doing (negative), I'm looking for

2

1 smoking, drinking; **2** missing; **3** surfing, getting; **4** spending; **5** writing

3

1f is leaving; **2**e am flying; **3**b are working; **4**c are getting; **5**d is having; **6**a Are you going

Spotlight on Grammar – Seite **17**

4

1 is checking; **2** is talking; **3** is calling; **4** are taking; **5** are putting; **6** am writing

5

1 am sitting; **2** Are you writing; **3** are you doing; **4** am enjoying; **5** Is it raining; **6** is raining; **7** is not raining; **8** am going; **9** are making; **10** are you coming; **11** am meeting; **12** is waiting

6

1 are you doing; **2** is he going; **3** am I speaking; **4** are you having; **5** Is it raining

7

1 I'm reading your email at the moment.
2 She's calling me soon.
3 Are you talking to Sharon later?
4 I'm looking at your photos now.
5 The phone is still ringing.
6 Is it snowing in Canada now?

8

1 just; **2** now; **3** just; **4** at the moment; **5** still

Spotlight on Grammar – Seite **18**

Contrast
Simple present ▶◀ present progressive

1

1 is coming, comes; **2** We play, we are playing; **3** sends, she's writing; **4** I'm driving, I often go; **5** work, aren't working, they're watching; **6** is cooking, we're eating

2

2 usually does; **3** never read; **4** am going; **5** is still waiting; **6** sells; **7** lies; **8** am playing; hidden signal word: normally

3

1 She always eats breakfast at 7.
2 It is snowing at the moment.
3 I love the summer.
4 Are you coming to the cinema with us tomorrow?
5 The train leaves at 4 o'clock.
6 I can't talk now. I'm washing my hair.

Spotlight on Grammar – Seite **19**

Test 1

1

1 newspapers, magazines; **2** dishes, sandwich; **3** hobbies, activities; **4** pairs of glasses, trousers; **5** homework, information

2

2 no article; **3** an; **4** an; **5** no article; **6** the; **7** no article; **8** the

3

1 its; **2** we; **3** your; **4** them; **5** mine; **6** hers; **7** ours; **8** theirs; **9** his; **10** yours

4

1 That, one; **2** This, one; **3** these, ones; **4** Those; **5** this, one, **6** this, that

Spotlight on Grammar – Seite **20**

5

1 I found an advert in the paper yesterday.
2 I'm looking for a job because I need the money.
3 Tomorrow I'm going for a job interview.
4 I want to buy myself a used laptop on the internet.
5 But laptops are always quite expensive.
6 My brother can't lend me the money.
7 He already gave some money to my sister.
8 I went to the cinema at the weekend.
9 I sent my sister an email but she still hasn't replied.
10 I am often at home earlier than my brother.

6

1 c; **2** f; **3** a; **4** e; **5** b; **6** d

7

1 There were; **2** There is; **3** there weren't; **4** There are; **5** There was; **6** There aren't; **7** There are; **8** There's

8

1 has; **2** doesn't have; **3** had; **4** have; **5** had; **6** don't have; **7** has

9

1 has; **2** does he have; **3** have; **4** has; **5** had; **6** don't have

10a

1 Do you have any brothers or sisters?
2 Did you have a good holiday last year?
3 Have you got a laptop?
4 Do you have time to help me with your homework?

10b

a3; **b**1/4; **c**2

Spotlight on Grammar – Seite **21**

11

1 Do you like your job as a hairdresser?
2 Do you earn enough money?
3 Does your boss give you enough help?
4 Do the customers think it is good?
5 What do you enjoy most?
6 What makes you happy?
7 What don't you like?
8 Do you get time off during the week?

12

2 doesn't; **3** don't; **4** doesn't; **5** don't; **6** doesn't; **7** don't; **8** doesn't

13

		just -ing	without -e	double letter
1	write		I'm writing	
2	win			I'm winning
3	visit	I'm visiting		
4	use		I'm using	
5	try	I'm trying		
6	take		I'm taking	
7	swim			I'm swimming
8	smile		I'm smiling	
9	sleep	I'm sleeping		
10	run			I'm running

14

1 are you doing; **2** I'm writing; **3** never use; **4** have to; **5** get; **6** am listening; **7** only see; **8** am meeting; **9** Do you want

Spotlight on Grammar – Seite **22**

8 Simple past

1

regular: watched, loved, killed, used, discovered, planned, enjoyed; irregular: was, told, became, were, was, grew up, saw, hurt, began, was, fought, won, read, was, thought, was

2

1 collected; **2** wanted; **3** loved; **4** preferred; **5** watched; **6** worried; **7** played

Spotlight on Grammar – Seite **23**

3

1 didn't like; **2** didn't have; **3** didn't play; **4** didn't want; **5** didn't try; **6** didn't enjoy

4

2 a; **3** f; **4** e; **5** b; **6** d

5

1 sang; **2** lost; **3** knew; **4** kept; **5** spent; **6** ate; **7** gave; **8** drove; **9** put

6

1 told, didn't tell; **2** knew, didn't know; **3** made, didn't make; **4** followed, didn't follow; **5** saw, didn't see

7

1 Did you buy; **2** Did Tom like; **3** did the criminals steal; **4** did Batman go; **5** Did Batman win

8

1 Batman decided to fight crime when he was young.
2 The criminals killed a lot of people.
3 Did you read Batman comics when you were at school?
4 My brother bought a Batman DVD yesterday.
5 A new Batman movie came out a few years ago.
6 Did Darren watch the new movie with you?
7 We went to see the film in the new cinema.
8 It was a very good film.

Spotlight on Grammar – Seite **24**

9 Present perfect

1

've just heard, has hurt, 've sent; 've never seen, haven't given, has killed, has also injured, has just arrived, have gone, have escaped, have arrested, hasn't been

infinitive	simple past	present perfect
hear	I heard	I've heard
hurt	I hurt	I've hurt
send	I sent	I've sent
see	I saw	I've seen
give	I gave	I've given
kill	I killed	I've killed
arrive	I arrived	I've arrived
go	I went	I've gone

2

1 A; **2** B; **3** A

Spotlight on Grammar – Seite **25**

3

1 've just come; **2** 've followed; **3** 've had; **4** 've not told; **5** has always been

4

1 The school hasn't cancelled …
2 Police haven't announced …
3 A reporter hasn't put videos …
4 The school hasn't asked …
5 We haven't heard …

5

1 Have you ever had trouble with guns at this school? No, we haven't.
2 Has the school been in the news before? Yes, it has.
3 Have you spoken to other reporters yet? No, I haven't.
4 Have you and your class ever discussed school shootings? Yes, we have.
5 Have you seen the therapist yet? No, I haven't.

6

1 for; **2** since; **3** for; **4** since; **5** since; **6** since

Contrast
Simple past ▸◂ present perfect

1

	When?	Since when?	For how long?	s.p.	p.p.
1	last weekend			✓	
2			for about five years		✓
3	last Monday			✓	
4		since May 15th			✓
5			for seven years		✓
6	two months ago			✓	

2

1 I've just finished; **2** We bought; **3** I've never heard; **4** lived; **5** has already made; **6** we played, we had; **7** Have you ever seen; **8** We've been

3

1 has brought; **2** drove; **3** I only paid; **4** I woke up; **5** I ate cornflakes; **6** I have been riding, for two hours; **7** My parents gave; **8** I have never spent; **9** We've lived in Hamburg for; **10** I've got stomachache. I've had stomachache for two days.

10 Past progressive

1

1 e; **2** c; **3** b; **4** d, **5** a

2

1 was sailing; **2** noticed; **3** was taking; **4** was moving, was trying; **5** was falling asleep, went

3

1 She was crying.
2 I was having breakfast.
3 Yes, I was (sleeping).
4 No, I wasn't (looking forward to stopping in South Africa).
5 I was writing a blog.

11 Past perfect

1

irregular: had been, had only been, had gone, had not had, had known, had told; regular: had looked, had tried, had pressed, hadn't asked

2

1 had come; **2** had given; **3** had prepared; **4** had told; **5** had pressed

3

2 drove, hadn't seen; **3** hurt, hadn't put on; **4** burned, had forgotten; **5** hurt, hadn't used; **6** broke, hadn't read

4

1 I had; **2** I hadn't; **3** I had; **4** I hadn't; **5** I hadn't

5

1 e had got up; **2** a hadn't worked; **3** d had done; **4** c had made; **5** b hadn't had

6

2 Sue had forgotten to wear a helmet so she hurt her head. / Because she had forgotten to wear a helmet, Sue hurt her head.

3 Mark had listened carefully so he did well. / Mark did well because he had listened carefully.
4 After/When Phil had washed his hands, he prepared the food.
5 After/When Suzi had cut the vegetables, she put them in the fridge.
6 When/After Jane had turned on the machine, she put in the pies.
7 Mike had forgotten to turn the computer off so Joe did it.
8 After/When Sarah had gone to work, the postman came.

Spotlight on Grammar – Seite **30**

12 Future

1

1 will bring; **2** will get; **3** will make; **4** will become; **5** will dry out

2

1 There will only be small cars.
2 There won't be as many fast cars.
3 Cars will cost much more.
4 You will have to pay much more for fuel.
5 There will still be too many cars on the road.
6 All cars will use electricity.
7 More people will share cars.
8 People won't drive cars any more.

Spotlight on Grammar – Seite **31**

3

1 will listen; **2** will protect; **3** will keep; **4** will put; **5** will check; **6** will know

4

1 is going to buy; **2** are going to put; **3** are not going to wait; **4** is going to take; **5** is not going to forget

5

1 will get; **2** are going to collect; **3** are going to use; **4** am not going to drive, will be; **5** 'll share

6

1 starts; **2** is going; **3** leaves, arrives; **4** is giving; **5** finishes; **6** is going

7

1 Scientists think that the greenhouse effect will make the earth warmer.
2 I'm going to an environment conference tomorrow.
3 The train arrives this evening at 7.
4 I'm going to be a scientist when I'm older.
5 I'm going to Spain next year.
6 I can't find my ticket. – I'll look for it.

Spotlight on Grammar – Seite **32**

Spotlight on... Question tags

1

1 don't they; **2** aren't you; **3** didn't you; **4** can't she; **5** don't you; **6** haven't you; **7** won't there; **8** don't we

2

1 does he; **2** have you; **3** do they, **4** was she; **5** were you; **6** have I; **7** was it; **8** can she

3

1 g; **2** f; **3** d; **4** b; **5** e; **6** h; **7** c; **8** a

4

2 You have a dog, don't you?
3 Your little brother starts school next year, doesn't he?
4 Faith hasn't seen the new film yet, has she?
5 Steven doesn't like football, does he?
6 You can play the piano, can't you?
7 Debbie won the competition last week, didn't he?
8 Carol has got a new car, hasn't she?

Spotlight on Grammar – Seite **33**

Test 2

1

just -ed	-ied	without -e	double letter
I belonged	I applied	I agreed	I fitted
I enjoyed	I buried	I argued	I grabbed
		I died	

2

1 spent; **2** Did you have; **3** was, **4** travelled; **5** visited; **6** didn't know; **7** met; **8** worked; **9** did you like; **10** showed; **11** told; **12** didn't stay

3

1 a; **2** b; **3** a; **4** b; **5** b; **6** b; **7** b; **8** b

4

1 did you call; **2** haven't called; **3** spoke; **4** was; **5** Has any-body seen; **6** gave; **7** has disappeared; **8** have just got; **9** sent

Spotlight on Grammar – Seite **34**

5

1 were sleeping; **2** was working; **3** was having; **4** was watching; **5** was ringing; **6** were still dreaming; **7** was eating; **8** were probably having; **9** were you doing; **10** was cleaning; **11** were probably getting; **12** were you riding

6

1	We went for a walk	2	s.p.
	after we had eaten.	1	p.p.
2	My brother phoned	2	s.p.
	when I had prepared everything for the party.	1	p.p.
3	When I had gone on holiday,	1	p.p.
	somebody broke into my house.	2	s.p.
4	I had just sat down on the sofa	1	p.p.
	when I heard the noise.	2	s.p.
5	When I came into the room,	2	s.p.
	the others had already started talking.	1	p.p.
6	After I had saved some money,	1	p.p.
	I bought a new TV.	2	s.p.

7

1 had gone; **2** had gone; **3** went; **4** went; **5** had gone; **6** had gone

8

1 had been; **2** had booked; **3** had packed; **4** had landed; **5** had talked; **6** had confirmed; **7** hadn't been; **8** hadn't expected

Spotlight on Grammar – Seite **35**

9

2 You will have a beautiful wife and two nice kids.
3 Your job will make you happy.
4 Many people will want to be your friends.
5 You will do sports regularly and you will always enjoy it.
6 You will travel around the world.

10

1 Ella is going to play tennis.
2 She isn't going to play table tennis.
3 Kira and Imran are going to play football.
4 They're not going to play basketball.
5 I'm going to go swimming.
6 I'm not going to go jogging.

11

1 will be; **2** will carry; **3** leaves; **4** am working; **5** am going; **6** will

12

1 d; **2** h; **3** e, **4** g; **5** a; **6** b; **7** c; **8** f

Spotlight on Grammar – Seite **36**

13 Modal verbs A

1

ability	**possibility**
I could give	I may even design
I was able to drive	I might even get
I can deal with	I could work
I'll be able to help	I could even start
I can speak	
Carpenters can work	

2

1 Where can florists work?
2 Can I work for myself as a travel agent?
3 Will I be able to take my dog to work?

Spotlight on Grammar – Seite **37**

4 Can bus drivers pick their favourite route?
5 Will I be able to bring my own tools?
6 Will I be able to use my French?

3

1 I can; **2** you may; **3** you can't; **4** you may; **5** you can't; **6** you can

4

1 was able to; **2** couldn't; **3** can; **4** can't; **5** might; **6** can't; **7** can; **8** may not

5

2 He could/might/may get a job there later.
3 He couldn't use the computer when he started.
4 He may/can answer some emails now.
5 He can understand what his colleagues are talking about now.
6 He may/might book a trip for himself soon!

6

1 Can/May I help you?
2 I can't use this tool.
3 I will be able to open my shop soon.
4 I couldn't hear you.
5 Could/Can you repeat that, please?
6 May I use the phone?
7 Tom can/may go home earlier today.
8 No one could / was allowed to leave the office.
9 May we smoke here?
10 Paula might/may learn German next year.

14 Modal verbs B

1

1 should; **2** should; **3** shouldn't; **4** should; **5** shouldn't; **6** should; **7** should; **8** should

2

1 had to; **2** Did he have to; **3** didn't have to; **4** has to; **5** will have to

3

1 mustn't; **2** don't have to; **3** don't have to; **4** mustn't; **5** mustn't; **6** don't have to

Spotlight on Grammar – Seite **39**

4

2 Jack doesn't have to talk; **3** He doesn't have to / needn't; **4** Jack doesn't have to work; **5** Jack has to work; **6** Jack doesn't have to work; **7** He has to use; **8** He doesn't have to

5

1 b; **2** h; **3** f; **4** d; **5** a; **6** g; **7** e; **8** c

6

1 don't have to / needn't; **2** have to/must; **3** mustn't; **4** should; **5** must; **6** don't have to/ needn't

7

1 May; **2** Could; **3** Should; **4** Do I have to; **5** has to; **6** must; **7** needn't; **8** shouldn't; **9** might; **10** Can I; **11** need to

Spotlight on Grammar – Seite **40**

15 Gerund

1a

1 cycling; **2** climbing; **3** skiing; **4** swimming; **5** diving; **6** running

1b

1 cycling; **2** running; **3** Swimming; **4** diving; **5** climbing; **6** skiing

Spotlight on Grammar – Seite **41**

1c

1 3; **2** 4; **3** 1, 2, 5, 6

2

1 The baseball player misses having fun.
2 The dancer enjoys looking good.
3 The tennis player keeps thinking about losing.
4 He imagines being the best runner in the world.
5 The football player mentions staying healthy.

3a

1 running; **2** running; **3** Winning; **4** losing; **5** looking; **6** Eating; **7** running; **8** worrying

3b

1 better at running; **2** worried about losing; **3** thinking about looking for; **4** looking forward to running

4

2 Suzi admitted taking drugs before the race.
3 Rob mentioned seeing Lucy after the race.
4 My mum recommended buying some new running shoes.
5 Rachel has stopped taking drugs.

5

1 in having fun; **2** at lying; **3** of getting; **4** about losing; **5** with being; **6** to taking

Spotlight on Grammar – Seite **42**

Contrast gerund ►◄ infinitive

1

1 being; **2** doing / to do; **3** to go; **4** in sailing; **5** having; **6** skiing; **7** learning / to learn; **8** playing; **9** to visit; **10** to take

2

1 a; **2** a/b; **3** a; **4** a/b; **5** b; **6** a

3

1 you want to buy; **2** is tired of listening; **3** don't remember seeing; **4** enjoy cooking; **5** suggest watching; **6** loves playing / to play; **7** is fed up with having; **8** stop laughing

Spotlight on Grammar – Seite **43**

Spotlight on ... Participles

1

1 dancing – present; **2** frozen – past; **3** screaming – present; **4** shocked – past; **5** crying – present; **6** worried – past

2

1 sleeping; **2** lost; **3** closed; **4** stolen; **5** waiting; **6** playing

3

1 The man dancing with my sister comes from Canada.
2 The shop opening on the High Street today sells sweets.
3 That's the skirt designed by Karl Lagerfeld.
4 Look at all the people standing in line at the baker's.
5 The number of car accidents caused by alcohol is rising.
6 That's the dress I want, the one hanging in the window.

Spotlight on Grammar – Seite **44**

16 Adjectives

1a

Samira: perfect, nice, nice, unattractive, big, plastic, most painful, terrible, normal, important; Helen: better, small, easy, horrible, new, same, perfect, better

1b

1 than; **2** as; **3** than; **4** as; **5** than; **6** as

Spotlight on Grammar – Seite **45**

2

1 uncomfortable; **2** intolerant; **3** impolite; **4** unsafe; **5** unemployed; **6** unfair; **7** illegal

3

2 big	bigger	biggest
3 easy	easier	easiest
4 hot	hotter	hottest
5 safe	safer	safest
6 thin	thinner	thinnest

4

1 most powerful; **2** friendlier; **3** worst; **4** best; **5** happier

5

1 fattest; **2** bigger; **3** ugliest; **4** more worried; **5** better

6

1 I'm the most perfect woman in the world.
2 I'm thinner than all the other women.
3 I've got the longest legs you've ever seen.
4 My name is the most beautiful name you've ever heard: Barbie!

7

1 My sister is more beautiful than me.
2 I think plastic surgery for teenagers should be illegal.
3 Richtig
4 Laura is the tallest but I'm taller than Jane.
5 Sarah is the shortest person in the class.

Spotlight on Grammar – Seite **46**

17 Adverbs

1

1 hard; **2** clearly; **3** long; **4** wrongly; **5** safely; **6** angrily; **7** slowly; **8** loudly; **9** easily; **10** well; **11** badly

2

1 The people there know the market well.
2 A travel agent explains things to you carefully.
3 A travel agent can book flights and hotel rooms more quickly than you.
4 A travel agent may sell you your trip more cheaply.
5 The customer can stay at home comfortably.
6 The customer can think about every detail carefully.
7 The customer can choose freely.
8 The customer may travel more cheaply.

Spotlight on Grammar – Seite **47**

3

1 cheaply; **2** safely; **3** easily; **4** carefully; **5** slowly; **6** simply

4

1 happily; **2** excitedly; **3** loudly; **4** perfectly; **5** badly; **6** well

5

1 The motorway was very busy.
2 However Jeremy and Emma arrived at the airport early.
3 They went to a coffee bar quickly for a sandwich.
4 Jeremy bought a cheap map of Berlin.
5 Suddenly it was rather late and they waited nervously to get on the plane.
6 They found their seats on the plane easily.

6

1 faster; **2** more cheaply; **3** much longer; **4** earlier; **5** more quickly

7

1 loud, loudly; **2** well, good; **3** soft, softly; **4** nice, nicely; **5** bad, badly; **6** happy, happily

Spotlight on Grammar – Seite **48**

Test 3

1

1 I couldn't / wasn't able to find my keys this morning.
2 Adam won't be able to leave school next year.
3 My sister was able to go surfing last summer.
4 I can't play the piano but I can play the guitar.
5 Linda won't be able to come to London tomorrow.
6 My parents weren't able to phone me two days ago.
7 Mr New will be able to have a day off next weekend.
8 We were able to buy a car yesterday.

2

1 May I; **2** Could he; **3** Can she; **4** Will we; **5** Can they; **6** Can you

3

1 may; **2** could; **3** might; **4** mustn't; **5** needn't

4

1 John should / has to wear a suit at work because he works in a bank.
2 You needn't count all the apples. Just weigh them.
3 Ray, you shouldn't work every weekend. You really need a break.
4 Should/Shouldn't I talk to my boss about the bullying?
5 Do you have to travel a lot in your new job?

5

1 must/should/have to; **2** shouldn't/ mustn't; **3** needn't; **4** needn't / doesn't have to; **5** should/must; **6** must

Spotlight on Grammar – Seite **49**

6

2 Collecting comics is my hobby.
3 Playing beach volleyball is great in the summer.
4 Dreaming about a good job is not enough.
5 Checking the machines is part of my job.
6 Writing a daily blog isn't easy.
7 Riding a horse is difficult.
8 Reading books is boring.

7

2 Because I'm fed up with playing basketball.
3 Because I'm worried about hurting my leg.
4 Because I'm thinking of going into town.
5 Because I'm good at talking to kids.
6 Because I'm tired of playing ice hockey all the time

8

1	I miss cooking	✔	I miss to cook	
2	I expect arriving		I expect to arrive	✔
3	she hates dancing	✔	she hates to dance	✔
4	they start smoking	✔	they start to smoke	✔
5	I promise coming		I promise to come	✔
6	she seems dreaming		she seems to dream	✔
7	you like drawing	✔	you like to draw	✔
8	I want going		I want to go	✔
9	he keeps talking	✔	he keeps to talk	
10	she agrees helping		she agrees to help	✔

9

1 losing; **2** to make / making; **3** to start; **4** swimming; **5** going out; **6** playing; **7** to move; **8** to listen / listening

10

1 changing; **2** copied; **3** stopped; **4** sitting; **5** broken; **6** chosen

Spotlight on Grammar – Seite **50**

11

2 Oslo is colder than Madrid.
3 Cindy isn't taller than Alice.
4 Fruit is healthier than chocolate.
5 The new film isn't as romantic as the old film.
6 My mother is as nervous as my father.
7 My sister is younger than me.
8 Comics are not more popular than youth magazines.

12

1 the best; **2** the most exciting; **3** the cheapest; **4** the most important; **5** the most difficult; **6** the worst

13

1 nervously; **2** well; **3** badly; **4** easily; **5** fast; **6** wonderfully

14

1 nervously; **2** bad; **3** wrong; **4** nervous; **5** badly; **6** wrong

15

2 Tom jogs longer than Tim.
3 Tom sings more beautifully than Tim.
4 Tom plays football better than Tim.
5 Tom shouts more loudly than Tim.
6 Tom is friendlier than Tim.

Spotlight on Grammar – Seite **51**

18 Relative clauses

1

2 Lucy is the girl who sorts our mail.
3 Mr Taylor is the man who organizes our meetings.
4 Meg and Ryan are the people who clean the office.
5 My boss is the woman who drives the blue car.

2

2 Phil brought in some cake which/that everybody liked.
3 Becky wrote an email which/that was in German.
4 I talked to some customers who/that were French.

3

1, 3, 4, 5

4

1 who/that; **2** not necessary; **3** which/that; **4** not necessary; **5** who

Spotlight on Grammar – Seite **52**

19 Quantifiers A

1

1 Some – einige; **2** every – jede/r; **3** all the – alle die; **4** each – jede/r (einzelne/r); **5** any – kein

2

1 Nicht jedes Modell; **2** Einige Modells; **3** sie haben keine Probleme; **4** Einige Fotografen; **5** alle die Fernsehwerbungen

Spotlight on Grammar – Seite **53**

3a

1 any; **2** some; **3** any; **4** some; **5** any; **6** some

3b

1 some, **2** any; **3** some; **4** any; **5** any; **6** any

4

1 somebody; **2** anywhere; **3** somewhere; **4** something; **5** anybody; **6** anything

5

1 right; **2** wrong; **3** right; **4** right; **5** right

6

1 all the; **2** all; **3** all the; **4** all of us, **5** all; **6** all the

7

1 Every girl wants to become a supermodel.
2 Some boys would also like to work as a model.
3 But not every model can be a supermodel.
4 All the fashion models are much too thin.
5 Model agencies look for all kinds of models.
6 They want models for every/each part of the body.
7 Ears, eyes, feet, hands – there are models for all parts of the body.
8 Would you like to look at some agency websites?

Spotlight on Grammar – Seite **54**

20 Quantifiers B

1

1 a lot of people; **2** few people; **3** much money; **4** a little money

2

1 many; **2** much; **3** much, **4** many; **5** much; **6** many

Spotlight on Grammar – Seite **55**

3

1 many; **2** much; **3** many; **4** many; **5** A lot of; **6** many

4

1 Comic Relief raises more money than other charities.
2 Red Nose Day is more famous than other charity events.
3 Most people wear red noses on Red Nose Day.
4 Comic Relief sells more red noses than Red Nose Day T-shirts.
5 Most children have fun on Red Nose Day.

5

1 little; **2** few; **3** little; **4** few; **5** few; **6** little

6

1 fewer; **2** less, **3** fewest; **4** least; **5** Few; **6** little

7

1 a few problems – einige Probleme; **2** a little help – etwas Hilfe; **3** very few ideas – sehr wenige Ideen; **4** A few ideas – einige der Ideen; **5** little time – (nur) wenig Zeit; **6** a few more people – ein Paar mehr Leute

Spotlight on Grammar – Seite **56**

21 Prepositions

1

→ **1** near; **3** above; **6** between; **7** through; **10** in; **11** outside; **12** past

↓ **2** after; **4** behind; **5** against; **8** on; **9** at

2

1 through; **2** at; **3** to; **4** behind; **5** out of

Spotlight on Grammar – Seite **57**

3

1 under; **2** on; **3** between; **4** at; **5** in; **6** behind

4

1 before; **2** till; **3** after; **4** since; **5** ago; **6** during

5

1 at; **2** in; **3** in; **4** on; **5** at; **6** on

6

1 with; **2** without; **3** for; **4** from; **5** about; **6** like

7

1 since 2006; **2** a few days ago; **3** since August; **4** since 2 o'clock; **5** for five years; **6** two months ago

Spotlight on Grammar – Seite **58**

22 Conditional sentences

1

1 won't look for another job; **2** will invite them to my party; **3** won't stay at the firm; **4** will buy her a car; **5** will wear his best clothes; **6** will help me find a job

2

1. I will have to travel a lot if I get the job as a saleswoman.
2. If I earn enough money, I can buy a better car.
3. I will need lots of clothes if I have to stay in hotels all the time.
4. If I spend more money on clothes, I won't have enough for food.
5. I won't have time for sports if I have to travel all the time.
6. If I get up early enough, I can go jogging.
7. If I get a new job, I will go on holiday to Barbados next year.
8. I will learn lots of new things if I go to this seminar.

3

1 b; **2** b; **3** b

Spotlight on Grammar – Seite **59**

4

1 worked; **2** found; **3** came; **4** were; **5** had; **6** went

5

1 isn't; **2** didn't have to; **3** were; **4** knew; **5** think; **6** had; **7** comes; **8** are

6

1 will phone; **2** were; **3** will use; **4** would speak; **5** will miss

7

1 had applied, would have got; **2** had worked, wouldn't have had; **3** had known, would have chosen; **4** had repaired, would have saved; **5** had told, wouldn't have done

8

1 wouldn't have known; **2** would be; **3** will find; **4** wouldn't have gone; **5** would help; **6** will be able to

Spotlight on Grammar – Seite **60**

23 Reported speech

1

1 this is the best time of her life; **2** he has met; **3** she really hopes she'll be able; **4** he can play the guitar now

Spotlight on Grammar – Seite **61**

2

1 if she could spend; **2** where it was; **3** how many teenagers would be there; **4** if the teenagers came; **5** what age they would be; **6** if they offered lots of activities at the camp; **7** how much it would cost

3

1 the day before; **2** that day; **3** the next day; **4** that evening

4

1 told; **2** tell; **3** says; **4** said; **5** said; **6** told

5

1 had been; **2** had met; **3** were; **4** would probably go; **5** had started; **6** couldn't

6

1 Charlie wrote that camp was the best way to spend the summer.
2 Rose said that she really hoped she could come again.
3 Mike wrote that he was listening to the camp song.
4 Silvia said that she had had such a great time.
5 Sagiv said that he hadn't got the camp DVD.
6 Eddie wrote that he had just received the DVD.
7 Debby said that he had just had an email from Tommy.
8 Tina said that we would be able to see the DVD on the camp website.

Spotlight on Grammar – Seite **62**

24 Passive

1

2 I was sent – ich wurde geschickt; **3** I was asked – ich wurde gefragt; **4** I was given – mir wurde gegeben; **5** I was told – mir wurde gesagt; **6** the old man was found – der alter Mann wurde gefunden; **7** I was chosen – ich wurde ausgewählt; **8** we were caught – wir wurden gefangen

2

1 was visited; **2** was told

Spotlight on Grammar – Seite **63**

3 was taught; **4** were also offered; **5** was given; **6** was introduced

3

1 was given; **2** was spent; **3** had been owned; **4** had been painted, were bought; **5** were hired

4

1 b; **2** b; **3** a; **4** a; **5** b; **6** b

5

1 The meals in the restaurant are prepared by prisoners.
2 The restaurant can be booked for birthday parties.
3 Joel's restaurant was mentioned in an article last week.
4 The restaurant was given a good review in the article.
5 Joel's restaurant has just been voted 'Best restaurant of the year'.
6 A second restaurant will be opened next year.

6

2 is closed; **3** can be ordered; **4** is required; **5** is served

Spotlight on Grammar – Seite **64**

Test 4

1

1 which/that; **2** which/that; **3** who/that; **4** which/that; **5** who/that

2

1 I'm going to save the money that I earn for a new bike.
2 Lou designs T-shirts that sell quite well.
3 The trees that are growing in this garden are very old.
4 Karen is the colleague who I admire most.
5 Pete is the boy who I like best in my class.
6 Josh is driving the car that Mike sold him.
7 Mel is the colleague who helps everybody.
8 The woman who answered the phone seemed young.

3

1 some; **2** somewhere; **3** any; **4** any; **5** any; **6** some; **7** some; **8** anybody

4

1 Can you give me some help please?
2 I don't have any money.
3 Richtig
4 I've got hardly any time this week.

5

1 every; **2** each; **3** each; **4** every; **5** every; **6** each

6

	All	All the	
1	✔		cars are bad for the environment.
2		✔	new cars that I've heard of use less petrol.
3	✔		houses need fresh paint from time to time.
4		✔	houses in this street are old.
5		✔	customers on this list have to be called.
6	✔		customers will have to wait a bit.
7	✔		firms have had a difficult year.
8		✔	firms in our area are struggling.

7

1 many; **2** more; **3** much; **4** many; **5** much, **6** Most

Spotlight on Grammar – Seite **65**

8

1 few; **2** a few; **3** a little; **4** little; **5** fewer; **6** few

9

1 behind; **2** under; **3** outside; **4** out of; **5** down; **6** through

10

1 for; **2** from; **3** during; **4** within; **5** since; **6** ago

11

1 at; **2** in; **3** on; **4** on; **5** in; **6** at; **7** on; **8** on

12

2 If Phil lived in California, he would be a rich man.
3 If Jane had lots of money, she would give it to poor children.
4 If Luke didn't play in a band, he wouldn't be very happy.
5 If Matt weren't Lisa's boyfriend, Sarah would go out with him.

13

1 What would you buy if someone gave you £100?
2 If there is a good film on TV on Saturday night, I'll stay at home.
3 Dennis would wear his best suit if he were invited for an interview.
4 If I had more time, I'd stay longer.
5 If the best MP3 player is too expensive, I'll buy a cheaper one.

Spotlight on Grammar – Seite **66**

14

1 e; **2** f; **3** g; **4** d; **5** a; **6** c; **7** h; **8** b

15

1 Joe said that he was repairing his car that afternoon.
2 My colleagues said that they had worked till 7 p.m. the day before.
3 Ms Keanes said that she would take the train to London the next day.
4 My boss asked me if I was going on holiday the following month.
5 Kylie said that she was phoning her mum that night.

16

1 was
2 had seen
3 would
4 was
5 had talked
6 went

17

1 was served
2 was cleaned
3 were put
4 was sent

18

1 The thief was seen in town last week.
2 Careful! This fence has just been painted.
3 The room had just been cleaned when we arrived.
4 My bike was repaired last week.

19

1 I was asked
2 Tim was asked
3 I was given
4 This cream isn't used